Ignite CALM

Achieving Bliss in Your Work

Debra J. Snyder, PhD
Doctor of Philosophy, Metaphysics

Foreword by Lisa McCourt

Copyright © 2014 by Debra J. Snyder

NorLightsPress
762 State Road 458
Bedford IN 47421

All rights reserved. No part of this book may be reproduced or transmitted in any form or by any means, electronic or mechanical, including photocopying, recording, or by any information storage and retrieval system, without written permission from the author, except for the inclusion of brief quotations in a review.

Printed in the United States of America

ISBN: 978-0-9906862-2-4

Cover Design by Debra Snyder and Vorris Justesen
Book Design by Nadene Carter
Edited by Sammie L. Justesen

First printing, 2014

Featuring CALM Conscious Collaboration Exercises With . . .

◆ David B. Goldstein ◆ Jennifer Crews ◆ Elizabeth Harper
◆ Deane Driscoll ◆ Tam Veilleux ◆ Lynne McGhee
◆ Sunny Dawn Johnston ◆ Dede Eaton ◆ Sue Yarmey
◆ Evelyn Rysdyk ◆ Suzanne Silvermoon ◆ Lisa Holcomb

Foreword by Lisa McCourt

Praise for *Ignite CALM*

"As is her style, Dr. Debra Snyder sheds a powerful beam of light on a topic important to your well-being. There is no need to be disappointed in your work and personal life. Get ready to be inspired! There is hope and power in *Ignite CALM*."

—Paul Coleman, Psy.D., Author
Finding Peace When Your Heart is in Pieces

"This book is a must read for anyone struggling with the demands of today's work environment. It is filled with powerful and practical ways to gain clarity around what YOU need to be happy. Deb takes you through a path of personal discovery which ends with the ability to make more conscious choices and lead a happier, more fulfilled life."

—Lynne McGhee
Fulfillment Coach, Lynne McGhee Coaching and Performing

"Having personally worked jobs in the education, medical, and corporate professions, I know this book speaks directly to the heart and soul in each of us. Deb Snyder's simple CALM formula is brilliant and essential across all working environments. You will discover this book to be the very change you were looking for."

—Jennifer Crews M.A.
Speaker, Author, Intuitive Guide & Mentor

"*Ignite CALM* is a beautifully written guidebook for living authentically and creatively in a state of eternal bliss. A pioneer on many levels, Deb Snyder's words masterfully navigate the reader through a map of personal development strategies toward the achievable destination of ultimate happiness."

—Elizabeth Harper
Metaphysical Artist, Color Clairvoyant, and
author of *Wishing: How to Fulfill Your Heart's Desires.*

"*Ignite CALM: Achieving Bliss in Your Work* is a fabulous book filled with golden nuggets of wisdom. This book will give you the tools to let go of the hard way and embrace grace, ease and CALM."

—Sunny Dawn Johnston, Bestselling Author of
The Love Never Ends - Message from the Other Side

"Deb's book is a breath of spiritual air in our corporate dis-embodied world. She creates a clear, inspiring guide for you to reclaim your spirit and remember your life purpose, even if it's while you're still collecting your corporate paycheck. It will teach you to thrive both materially and spiritually."

—Paulette Kouffman Sherman, author of
Dating from the Inside Out, When Mars Women Date
and *The Cancer Path*

Dedication

I lovingly dedicate this book to the worker bees.
Without you, we would not taste the honey of life.
We could not exist.

Preface

The details presented here are accurate and truthful to my direct experience and perception. I have, however, changed descriptions, names, and locations in some circumstances to protect the identity and privacy of the actual people involved. I chose not to name the specific company that provided the catalyst for this book, as I believe they merely represent a widespread problem in our places of work. Every day, countless people face hostile and energetically unhealthy environments that can chip away at their very souls. My sincere wish is for these stories to open the hearts and minds of people and begin making positive shifts in how we work and live in this world. Conscious change begins with each of us.

Acknowledgements

I would like to express my sincere gratitude to the many sensational people who have been a constant support in my life and helped with the manifestation of this book. To my husband Mark, who is a devoted source of love and encouragement, and has an unyielding belief in my ability to make a difference for others. To my gorgeous daughter Raegan, for always sharing her pure essence and joy. You make Mommy smile every day and I am so proud of you. My love and appreciation to my parents, family, and family of friends. I am truly blessed. To Penny Belleville for being such a caring sounding board and a true friend. To David Nicholson for your loving generosity, stellar skills, and masterful humor. To the sensational *Ignite CALM Conscious Collaborators* who contributed exercises for this book; you are a powerful force of good and I am blessed to know you all. To Lisa McCourt, for being the most generous and authentic person I know. To Dee Justesen, Sammie Justesen, and my publishing family at NorLightsPress; thank you for believing in me and helping me share this knowledge with the world. To my HeartGlow Center family and all the fabulous contributors to *Inner Tapestry Journal* and *Transform*; may we continue to shine our hearts together forever more. I love you all.

Remember that the Hidden Power within us pulls the strings;
There is the guiding Force, there is the life,
There, one might say, is the man himself.
Never think of yourself as a mere body with its various appendages;
The body is like the ax of a carpenter:
Dare we think that the ax is the carpenter himself?
Without this Inner Cause, which dictates both action and inaction,
The body is of no more use than the weaver's shuttle without a weaver,
The writer's pen without a writer,
Or the coachman's whip without a horse and carriage.

Honor the highest thing in the Universe;
It is the Power on which all things depend;
It is the Light by which all of life is guided.

Honor the highest within yourself; for it, too,
Is the Power on which all things depend,
And the Light by which all life is guided.

Dig within. Within is the well-spring of Good;
And it is always ready to bubble up, if you just dig.

—Marcus Aurelius (121-180 AD)

Contents

Foreword. 1

Chapter 1: Ignite CALM 5

Chapter 2: Creativity 19

Chapter 3: Authenticity 35

Chapter 4: Luminosity 51

Chapter 5: Mindfulness. 67

Chapter 6: Simplicity. 81

Chapter 7: Money & Abundance 95

Chapter 8: Carrying the Torch of Leadership 109

Chapter 9: Conscious Collaboration 121

CALM Conscious Collaboration Exercises 122

About the Author 159

Foreword
by Lisa McCourt

Creativity. Authenticity. Luminosity. Mindfulness.

TOGETHER THEY COMPRISE Deb Snyder's formula for a transformed work environment, one in stark contrast to those most commonly encountered today. Deb is a visionary—a maverick world-changer who has experienced the realities of the contemporary workplace and identified the critical ingredients required for its evolution.

With great insight, courage, and a splash of sass, Deb has created a roadmap for those of us who are ready for a new paradigm, not just in our careers, but in the whole experience of our day-to-day living. You may have heard the axiom popular in self-growth circles that "how we do one thing is how we do all things." It means that our experience of the myriad facets of our lives stems always from our experience of ourselves. In the context of *Ignite CALM* then, how we relate to our jobs is merely one extension of how we relate to life itself.

For example, when you endure a turbulent, unsatisfying romantic love relationship and abandon it to go directly into relationship with a new partner, what typically happens? We all know the answer. Without taking the necessary steps to grieve, understand, and process the initial relationship—without discovering what we can learn from it and where we can take responsibility for it—we will recreate the identical flavors of discontent with a new partner. The same is true for people who reactively jump from one employment situation to the next, always blaming company policy or their employers for their dissatisfaction, always romanticizing the new position as the long-awaited answer to their employment prayers, and inevitably becoming quickly disillusioned and unsatisfied again.

This book breaks the cycle. It not only offers invaluable, well-researched information for employers, but also teaches readers how to change their own game instead of perpetually expecting their next manager to change the game for them.

One way Deb interrupts this ubiquitous loop is by advocating the powerful question, "How can this situation be made better, not just for me, but for all workers everywhere?" Naturally, training ourselves to habitually frame questions in this context rolls out the welcome mat for divine guidance and opens us to the best possible solutions and outcomes.

I wish this book had been around in my early employment years as I climbed the publishing industry's editorial ladder, famously fraught with dizzying displays of house-hopping, title-swapping, mergers, and the lightning-quick birth and death of imprints. I don't recall any of these spirit-based, anciently wise concepts being discussed at BookExpo, American Library Association conferences, or author-launch cocktail parties at the major houses. I doubt that they're discussed widely and openly in any industry, and that is a shame.

From her insights on connecting to our deepest wisdom and finding genuine purpose in our work to her insistence on moral excellence, never-ending personal growth, and the need for conscious leaders to light the way, Deb fiercely and fearlessly directs our gaze into a future of immense benefit to us all. The four ideals represented by her CALM acronym have the potential to dramatically revolutionize the world we live in and the manner in which we contribute meaningfully to it.

Whether you feel overworked, underutilized, underappreciated, or all of the above, you'll find immediate relief in this timely volume. By shining healing light on the outdated and egregiously unproductive corporate systems that have plagued individuals, companies, and entire industries far too long, it illuminates a hopeful path toward a bright new consciousness for businesses of all shapes and sizes.

Underscoring her position on conscious collaboration, Deb includes contributions of exercises, meditations, and energy-shifting modalities from a dozen talented holistic practitioners and self-development experts, many of these providing springboards for further absorption of the *Ignite CALM* principles. Deb's emotionally courageous sharing of her own employment difficulties inspires deep inner reflection and reinforces the need for rigorous honesty with one's self. Her thoughtful questions inspired me to closely examine where I've been in my work life, where I am now, and where I hope to go.

Want to know what makes Deb Snyder the perfect messenger for this powerful workplace-restructuring formula? She's creative. She's authentic. She's luminous. And she's mindful. Tomorrow's leaders and policy-makers, as well as tomorrow's workers—whatever color their collars, would do well to heed the joyful advice she puts forth in this elegant, smart, and practical volume.

I've found that often a book will appear at precisely the moment it's most needed in a reader's life. I hope this is one of those books for you.

—Lisa McCourt, award-winning ghostwriter,
writing coach, and bestselling author of
many books including *I Love You, Stinky Face* and
Juicy Joy – 7 Simple Steps to Your Glorious, Gutsy Self

Chapter One
Ignite CALM

"Your time is limited, so don't waste it living someone else's life. Don't be trapped by dogma, which is living with the results of other people's thinking. Don't let the noise of others' opinions drown out your own inner voice. And most important, have the courage to follow your heart and intuition."
—Steve Jobs

LET'S FACE IT—MOST PEOPLE need to work for a living. Although retiring at age fifty to run a small bistro in a quaint town is a tantalizing idea, the fact is, most of us work in small businesses, large corporations, civil service, busy stores, or high-production manufacturing environments. There's nothing wrong with a life filled with good, steady work. However, challenges arise when making a living takes priority over creating a loving, meaningful life.

This book explores how each of us can embrace conscious business qualities, bring our best selves to work every day, and discover true happiness while on the job—no matter what the job.

Going to work when you hate your job (or even mildly dislike it) can eat away at your happiness. Perhaps you're stuck with a bad manager, unpleasant co-workers, a heavy workload, a job that's tedious beyond belief, or you're resentful about a pay cut. I could list a dozen more reasons for being unhappy at work, but I suspect you know all of them.

The advice and practical guidance I present in *Ignite CALM: Achieving Bliss in Your Work* is for those who want to improve their lives and take positive action to attain success at work, at home, and in relationships. I believe these techniques and lessons will help you transform your life and develop an exceptional understanding of yourself. I will approach things holistically, looking at all angles, to help you identify and meet your professional and personal goals.

Everything in life is connected. We can't expect to live happy lives if we're miserable at work. Not only do we spend about 50 hours per week at our jobs, we end up wasting precious energy complaining about work during our off hours. This often leads to frustration and disappointment with our friends and family who've heard it all, again and again. Yet, within us, we each have the power to create working lives that are both pleasant for us and profitable for our employers. It's up to us to make changes, and those changes begin in our own hearts and actions.

Together, let's break the negative habits and find a new way of being. Let's ignite CALM!

What do I mean by "ignite?" I mean this is the moment to LIGHT IT UP and stoke your inner fire by taking positive action—by accepting responsibility for your own life and how you live it.

We decide where we work and we choose the people we spend our time with. Don't fall into the comfortable trap of blaming people and things outside yourself for your unhappiness. "Oh, I'd be so happy if it wasn't for this crappy job, grumpy parent, or controlling spouse."

Enough already! This is your life and it can be anything you want—if you have the courage to genuinely be yourself in every moment. This is what I want for you: empowerment and unyielding bliss in your life.

Some of you may be thinking, "Yeah, right. What does this spiritual chick know about working hard for a living to pay bills and deal with stress?"

Well, this spiritual chick, actually I prefer "energy chick," attended the school of hard knocks and I've had more than my fair share of jobs during thirty years in the workforce. Some were good, some bad, and some were a means to an end—a way of achieving another goal. I grew up in a relatively poor to lower middle-income family where we never got anything unless we worked for it. No silver spoons at our family table; more like the plastic "sporks" you find in fast food restaurants that come pre-wrapped with a napkin and maybe some salt and pepper packets.

In addition to my current profession as an author and speaker, I have flipped burgers, waited tables, tended bar, worked in human resources placing people in manufacturing positions, been a workers compensation insurance adjuster, a telemarketer, manned an advice phone line, been a gift shop owner, a writer, an editor, a spiritual counselor, an executive director of a non-profit, and my favorite job of all—being a mom.

Being a parent is a fabulous responsibility and a blessing that requires a great deal of work. Parenting is as valuable as any paid position in our society. If you're a stay-at-home parent, give yourself credit for never leaving the workforce, because you accepted a rewarding—and challenging task—a job that never ends. This book is as much for you as for the nurse, teacher, factory worker, or corporate leader. We all understand hard work and each of us can find a profession, a calling that aligns with our Divine purpose.

The idea for this book came to me when I recently spent twelve frustrating weeks in the trenches of corporate America being trained to manage claims for a Fortune 500 insurance company. Although I have an extensive background in claims, I've been self-employed for the past dozen years and home with my daughter, Raegan, who has profound special needs. Working from home gave me the advantage of personal freedom and the ability to function in blocks of time, with projects and events often scheduled months in advance. I was blessed to work barefoot, in yoga pants as I wrote articles, spoke with clients by phone, and pitched my next project to producers and event organizers. I also had the disadvantage of a weird schedule and inconsistent pay, which many artists, writers, and performers can relate to. My husband's job was more traditional and provided a steady income flow and benefits. When his work shifted suddenly with the relocation of his employer, he became unemployed. Feeling the need to secure benefits and a steady check, we both put out resumes and were open to what the Universe brought our way. You guessed it ... the Universe brought me to Hell, disguised as a cubicle.

At the time I was between writing and teaching projects, so I thought returning to the corporate workplace for a bit might be a fun change of pace, while giving my husband an opportunity to work from home and spend time with our daughter. We basically switched roles to prevent each other from burning out. I felt I could still do my writing and spiritual work and help keep things stable at home. Little did I realize this jaunt back into big business would have me crash and burn, a racecar headed for the wall at full speed in a collision that would lead me to a greater understanding of the circumstances and suffering of others.

Now allow me make to this clear: For many years I've worked in the business world as a touring author, speaker, and metaphysical teacher. After traveling the world meeting thousands of people and appearing onstage at conferences and on numerous radio shows, Internet broadcasts, and even national television, I know marketing, I know communication, and I know people. In fact, I love people and their diverse perspectives and reflections. I have enjoyed negotiating contracts and representing myself and many other companies in the mind-body-spirit genre in a professional capacity. I say all this because I want you to recognize I'm not naïve to the ways of business and have seen the best and worst of people on full display. Trust me, working with the media requires a certain thickness of skin and determined resilience. Just ask my publicist.

Believing my full and creative life would provide a strong foundation for my new employer, I eagerly accepted a position as a benefits specialist and bought some shoes to cover my bare toes.

Those same shoes would be on my feet as I was escorted out of the building 82 days later with tears streaming down my cheeks and my few personal possessions stuffed into a cardboard box.

"Not a good fit," they told me after I raised concerns about the ethics of the job and significant stress of the work environment. In my short time there, my blood pressure had gone through the roof, my weight was up eight pounds, and I felt overwhelmed and tearful from the pressure. I witnessed many of my co-workers going through the same struggles, some even vomiting from anxiety and tension. The company was filled with many wonderful people, working hard, yet the overall mood seemed severe and lacked smiles. More than one person looked at me strangely for smiling and saying hello when we passed in the hall. The energy of the place was dense and hurried, with harsh lighting and fierce lines. My manager didn't wish to hear my opinion and felt I was "taking too much time to care" about the people whose claims I worked on. I needed to detach and speed up ... or find the door back home. Ugh! At that point, I agreed with them. I was not a good fit. No one could ever pay me enough to not care. In this life, I answer to a higher calling ... and it certainly wasn't there.

The awkward job fit wasn't a total surprise to everyone. In fact, many of my friends who were already working in a corporate environment were flabbergasted I even considered doing such work. Admittedly, I'm an eclectic person and a free thinker. I have a big heart and a big mouth and have never been afraid to use either. Live and let live. Conceived in the Summer of Love and born under the sign of Pisces, I have a bit of my parents' hippie nature in my blood. Why did I expect myself to adopt the behavior of a traditional work environment? And why did I expect them to accept me—a woman with crystals and essential oils adorning her cubicle?

I believed the union of a smart, successful person with a smart, successful company would naturally be a great fit. It wasn't. Not because my skills and their requirements didn't match, but because we held different values and priorities. We simply did not resonate. No matter how hard I worked, it wasn't going to work for me to be there, so leaving was indeed best for all. When I agreed to take an opt out and leave the job voluntarily, I was told I would get two weeks severance pay and wished well, no hard feelings; a win-win. I was dismayed to learn the severance pay came with a multipage release and gag order. My inner hippie rose in protest. I told them to keep their severance, because I would never give up my freedom to speak about my experiences. I am a writer after all! Fear choked me when I realized I was depriving my family of needed funds for the sake of my principles and ethics. The Universe responded within a day with unexpected payments for past and future projects, checks from a variety of sources for both my husband and myself. The Universe was making sure we didn't feel a financial loss from doing the right thing for our souls.

Although this diversion into the corporate world caused me great discomfort, it also gave me a tremendous opportunity to be of service to others in a manner I hadn't considered before—by reaching out to other workers, regardless of their professions, and helping them cope with difficult environments and make positive changes in their lives. I was inspired to bring forth my holistic techniques and lessons to help people transform their professional lives and find greater happiness at work and at home.

To do this we must take action for ourselves. Even though people make the business world go round, the needs of the people are often the first to be neglected in business. If we take the responsibility of our work wellness into our own hands, then we are no longer at the mercy of a company that's too busy to care. We will care about ourselves, make better choices, and create environments truly worthy of working in.

You already realize I want you to get fired up—to IGNITE. We can't just "be calm" or "stay calm" like the cliché phrases printed on t-shirts. The sad fact is, in the workplace most people do not know or recognize how it feels to be calm or in a place of peace.

In my teachings, CALM is an acronym for essential components that allow bliss to work in your life. They are easy to apply on the job, at home, and for any challenge you face. When we ignite CALM, we make an active choice to bring the best of ourselves to whatever we're doing in that present moment.

CALM = Creativity, Authenticity, Luminosity, and Mindfulness

Ignite CALM is my call to action for all of us to find this special place within ourselves and look at the circumstances in our lives through this new, high vibration filter. As you move through the book, you'll learn how I define each component and how you can apply these concepts to your own life in that very moment.

- This technique will bring you closer to your inner calling and soul's purpose.
- You will no longer doubt your thoughts and actions.
- You will hear your inner voice loud and clear, enabling you to tune out static and confusion caused by the rules and projections of others.
- You will know you are in resonance with your purpose—and you will also know, with confidence, what no longer serves you and needs to be released.

Over the years many of my clients have felt great frustration about being unhappy, yet they didn't know what they wanted or needed to *be* happy. This program will help you align with your heart's desires, make positive choices, and unleash powerful changes to create the life you yearn for, supported by a job you love.

I want to share a story I rarely disclose, because it's so personal. That statement may seem odd for the fans and readers of my first book, *Intuitive Parenting*, in which I share many personal details about the health and well being of my child and myself. This is a different type of personal. This is a true story about money. I was taught from a young age that discussing money was rude, and besides, I never had enough money to talk about. Many people talked money; they knew the language and wanted to hear all about it. I learned one day what a potent teaching tool money can be when I casually mentioned to a group I was instructing about the time I made $50,000 in ten minutes.

I'd always considered this experience a matter of Angels or Divine guidance, so I didn't realize the amount of money involved would cause people to stop in their tracks. And that's exactly what happened in my small group that day.

"What are you talking about?" asked one woman. "Do you seriously believe $50,000 was sent to you from the Angels?" Her voice dripped with sarcasm.

"Well, it was sent to me from a company in California, but I do believe my guides had a hand in it. And either way, the bank accepted the money transfer!" I said with my own smug grin and a laugh.

I went on to tell them the story of when I was at a low point in my life, trying to cope with my daughter's immense medical problems and adjusting to no income after leaving my career to stay home with my girl. On top of all that, I just had major back surgery, a spinal fusion, and was still in a back cast. We had sold our home and moved into an old apartment to simplify and have fewer expenses. This seemed a long way to fall from the life we'd created years before. However, the decision to let go of the house and leave my job was driven from a place deep inside myself. I knew with all my being it was somehow going to work out. I just needed to be in the moment and keep listening to my heart.

Not long after my daughter was born, I purchased a series of domain names to create a small website that would spread awareness and show support for children with disabilities. One domain name in particular was of interest to a large company I used as a supplier for some of my products. They were quite surprised to discover a little mom from Maine owned the name. The company owner joked with me that I was lucky to register the name before his company did. The truth is, I was *inspired* to register it and did so after waking up with the idea one morning. Just as I was *inspired* to put that name up for auction a year or so later, while living in the worn apartment.

The inspiration to sell the name seemed right, because I thought I might make a few hundred dollars at a time we needed the money. I followed my instincts, sent out a few emails to appropriate leads, and waited to see if anything would come of it. The same day I received a phone call from the business owner who had lovingly teased me the year before. He wasn't interested in an auction, but he wanted to secure the name without question and offered me $50,000 for the five domain names I owned. I accepted his offer immediately over the phone, still wearing plaid pajamas and a back cast.

You can imagine how this windfall positively affected my family. When we released our attachment to money, it flowed in to us with little effort. We were able to put a down payment on an affordable home and eliminate debt so we could live on only one income. I could stay home and take care of my daughter without worrying about every penny. It changed our lives forever, as I went back to school to study metaphysics and went on to be writer, a self-development teacher—and now here I am, an award-winning author with my fourth book, doing what I can to help people around the world open their hearts to their own Light and align with their souls' calling.

Please realize how all things are connected. Every decision we make, every action we take moves us closer to, or further away from, our soul's purpose. In conscious reflection of this experience, I see the energy of it all and the beauty of it. I hope sharing my story at this time will help people be more open to the unbounded possibilities available to each of us. And yes, that can also mean money. I dedicate an entire chapter in this book to money and abundance. In that chapter we'll explore the energy behind abundance and examine how shifting your perspective with CALM can help you unlock the doors to unlimited wealth and happiness.

"Bloom where you are planted."
—The Bishop of Geneva, Saint Francis de Sales (1567-1622)

How to use this book

The material I present in this book is easy to use. I only ask that you open your heart and mind to alternative ways of thinking, and then take time to sort out how you feel about your work and your life. My methods help you do just that, and besides, you're worth it! Set aside the ingrained habits passed down to you by a society that often values money over people and process over integrity. When we ignite CALM we will strive to remain in the highest integrity and truth, even if the truth sometimes hurts and leads us away from a comfortable path we've become addicted to. You need not abandon things you truly believe are working in your life. Just be sure to leave room for things you may have never before considered.

You'll notice I often speak about "action," the simple act of doing something. Wishes, prayers, and intentions are important, yet they lose significance if you don't take decisive action toward your desires. That means viewing your relationship with the Universe as a two-way street. You and the Universe are co-collaborators in the amazing design of your life. Would I have received big money for the domain names if I hadn't taken steps to facilitate the sale? No, I wouldn't. I needed to follow up on my inspiration by taking positive, deliberate action in support of the energy of the situation. Together, the Universe and I made that payment a reality.

The challenge is—many of us don't take any action, positive or negative. We *wish*, we *want*, we *crave*, we *bitch*, and then we don't do a darn thing about it. We construct barriers to our success with negative attitudes and destructive behavior. We become our own worst enemies by sabotaging the seeds of our ideas before they can germinate and take root. Let's give ourselves room to grow.

As you make your way through this book, realize this is a process of personal growth and transformation. I am not giving you one-size-fits-all seeds of wisdom. I am giving you tools and a safe space to cultivate your own wisdom, all the while taking into account your unique environment and circumstances.

Ignite Calm is organized to first introduce you to the concepts in CALM and then provide examples of how they can successfully work in your life. Each chapter fully explores a topic and then presents helpful applications to help you gain practical understanding. The final section of the book is comprised of exercises and activities submitted by conscious collaborators—my self-improvement colleagues who are here to help stoke your fire. You'll find these activities fun and easy to use.

In the personal development genre we read fascinating tales of people who travel to distant lands to find themselves. As the sun rises on a gorgeous vista, they realize, upon deep reflection ... they were never missing in the first place. This is all poignant and romantic, but most of us don't get to take a year off to find our callings while meditating on a mountaintop. We work regular jobs and spend our free time in service to our families by attending Little League games, piano recitals, and medical appointments. As Saint Francis de Sales says, our challenge is to bloom where we're planted—to find our bliss at work, at home, and in each and every precious, messy moment of life.

As you read this book, you'll realize that projections are limiting. You'll learn to release limitations placed upon you by someone else's lack of vision or your own insecurity. You are more than your job; more than any problem. You are greater than how you currently perceive yourself. If you picked up this book, you are primed and ready for a new way of seeing. This is your inner journey—a trip that will be unique for each person, because each of us is one of a kind, exceptional and distinctive.

I promise you, we each have a purpose in life. Give yourself the gift of discovering that purpose. Find out how you're meant to be of service to the world. Find what makes you come alive.

Are you willing to truly open yourself and fully embrace the lessons in this book? Are you courageous enough to let your unique talents shine and be successful beyond all limitation?

I know you are.

Let us open ourselves to our inner fire.
Let's ignite CALM!

Ignition points

- Start a dialogue with yourself by journaling. The most important person you should be talking and listening to is—you!
- Reflect on your childhood and ask yourself, "What did I most want to be when I grew up? Why?"

Chapter One Exercise – Ignite CALM

The questions

In the next chapters you'll go through an in-depth exploration of the CALM components. This first exercise is a technique I'd like you to use whenever you face a decision or challenge.

This technique gets us into our best place, so we can see a situation clearly without distraction from the ego mind. These four questions are at the heart of the CALM approach—the only questions you need to get the internal fire started. This is your flash point, where you strike the match.

The inspired inquiry you're about to undertake will forever shift you. You will stop splashing in shallow water and move into the deep ocean of your own nature. As our knowledge of the CALM concepts expand, these questions will take on greater significance and meaning. You can do this exercise alone or in a group where you're discussing a common issue.

Ignite CALM:	To ignite CALM, ask yourself four simple questions and be absolutely honest in your answers.
Creativity:	Have I looked at this situation creatively?
Authenticity:	Am I being true to my personal values and goals?
Luminosity:	Am I bringing the best of me to this issue?
Mindfulness:	How does this situation affect my life and others?

Although these questions may seem basic, they are incredibly powerful. Think back over your life to critical decisions that didn't work out so well. Now apply the CALM questions in hindsight. During my life, I could have avoided a great deal of pain by asking these questions before I jumped into situations. Now, when I face decisions this simple exercise helps me find the proper place within. Give it a try right now with an issue you're currently facing at work or at home. Your answers will show where your opportunities live.

If you used my own corporate crisis as a sample, it might look something like this:

Ignite CALM:	To ignite CALM, ask yourself four simple questions and be absolutely honest in your answers.
Creativity:	Have I looked at this situation creatively? **You bet I have! I have tried everything to make this work. I think.**
Authenticity:	Am I being true to my personal values and goals? **Some of the things I need to do for my job don't support my life goals and beliefs. It doesn't feel right to me and I am starting to resent everything about this place!**
Luminosity:	Am I bringing the best of me to this issue? **To be honest, I started that way, but my performance seems to get worse as my frustration grows. No, I guess I'm not in my highest place.**
Mindfulness:	How does this situation affect my life and others? **Now that I think about it, I am the last thing this company was looking for. The job still needs to be done, whether I like it or not. It's their process, but it doesn't have to be mine unless I choose that option.**

My sample answers clearly show this job was not in alignment with my Authenticity component, which caused the problem to escalate further and bring out the worst in me instead of the best. Hard to admit, but it's always best to be honest with yourself. As I applied the full CALM method, I gained insight into my own behavior and its effects on the other party. I was able to make a decision that supported the interests of the company and myself. The method helped me take a deeper, honest look that led me to a conscious decision.

As you gain greater insight into the CALM components, you'll see how these four questions help you reach the heart of each situation, connect with your highest self, and make decisions that resonate with your life's purpose.

This is the starting point. Now let's go stoke that fire!

Chapter Two
Creativity

"An essential aspect of creativity is not being afraid to fail."
—Edwin Land

OH, NO! ON TOP OF THE PRESSURE to be efficient and productive at work, now Deb is asking us to get creative.

Relax. You're safe with me. Together we'll explore what it means to be creative at work and in our daily lives. This isn't a middle school art class, where the naturally gifted students are graced by the love and undivided attention of the teacher, while the rest of us struggle at a distant table trying to draw believable scenes. In my mind's eye I can still see my hand-like tree with a circular blob for leaves and a hole in the trunk for a bird to live. I drew that tree for years and it has taken me years to appreciate it with good humor.

What is creativity?

Not among the gifted artists, I was usually seated on the outskirts of the classroom getting frustrated while drawing, then erasing, then drawing, then erasing, always trying to hide my work because it paled in comparison to the many Rembrandts in my class. At the tender age of eleven, I had not yet found my own creative spark and I wore insecurity like a badge of dishonor.

Actually I did have a spark. I didn't realize at the time the ability to speak in front of others was also an art form, a channel for creative energy. I, like many other people, convinced myself I wasn't creative or artistic because I couldn't draw realistic pictures or play a musical instrument. Yearning for approval from authority figures, I did what I was told and allowed myself to be placed in labeled boxes. Not an artist. Not an athlete. Not a musician. What the heck was this kid?

Maybe just like you, this kid needed encouragement, a few less rules, and space to explore away from the pressure of a classroom. My natural creative self was being stifled and needed to find a form of expression. I soon discovered dance, theater, and public speaking—and I haven't stopped that party. Funny thing; looking back, I wasn't an especially celebrated writer in my youth, but now my love affair with the written word is a huge part of who I've become. By stepping away from preconceived ideas and labels, I discovered my own distinctive creative signature, which is ever evolving and on display in my choice of fashion, hobbies, and career.

Creativity, the first essential component in CALM, can be expressed in a myriad of ways, but it all distills down to our ability to *create*. When we create, we cause something unique to come into being that did not exist before: an expression of ourselves. I like the definition put forth by dictionary.com which states creativity is "the ability to transcend traditional ideas, rules, patterns, relationships, or the like, and to create meaningful new ideas, forms, methods, interpretations, etc." The "etc." is most pleasing to me, because it allows us to fill in our own blanks. And that's what creativity is to me—filling in the blanks and finishing the sentences of your life. It is the freedom to choose the color of your crayons, the beat in your groove, and the lover you lie with at night.

Do you remember playing *Mad Libs* in the car while on long road trips—those thick pads of paper embedded with themed stories waiting for our magic touch? Of course today, *Mad Libs* have morphed into digital apps and are no longer the dog-eared pages marked with inky fingerprints and snack food stains. The premise is still the same. Players select different nouns, adjectives, verbs, and adverbs to create a unique and often comical story. As we fill in the blanks and allow our creativity to flow, the stories become outlandish in our attempts to surpass our friends. Think of life itself as a fun, vibrant game of fill in the blanks. But instead of filling them with nouns and adverbs, we fill the blanks in our lives with choices, attitudes, and actions, each imbued with our energetic essence. We are creatively designing our life stories in each moment, with every step and breath.

If you choose a career in the arts, it's easy to see how creativity is an essential component for success. But what if you're a doctor, a lawyer, or a chimney sweep? A smile spreads across my face as I picture Bert, the lovable character portrayed by Dick Van Dyke in the Disney movie *Mary Poppins*. He was a chimney sweep with talent and creativity, a memorable character. I venture to guess most people in that profession whistle tunes as they do their dirty jobs. It's all in the attitude. Our ability to bring levity and a unique perspective to difficult situations determines our success and also our happiness. Bert could have complained with every sweep of the brush, yet doing a job joyfully, with a grin and a song, raised the vibration and increased production. Next time you have a messy job to do, think of Bert and hum a tune that lives in your heart.

The creativity gap

Scientific studies on creativity in the workplace reveal a creativity gap. Adobe's 2012 *State of Create*[1] global benchmark study revealed, "eight in ten people feel that unlocking creativity is critical to economic growth and nearly two-thirds of the respondents feel creativity is valuable to society, yet ... only one in four people believe they are living up to their own creative potential."

---

1   State of Create Study: Global Benchmark Study on Attitude and Beliefs about Creativity at Work, School and Home," Adobe, April 9, 2012, http://dld.bz/dyCRx

To obtain this information, the study conducted interviews of 5,000 adults across five countries, including Japan, Germany, France, the United Kingdom, and the United States. Of the respondents, 75 percent said they were under immense pressure to be productive rather than creative, with lack of time and money being the greatest barrier to creativity. Globally, we yearn to express our creativity and be more successful, yet we perceive we are denied access to the creative well, because breaking away from the chains of conventional thought is too expensive or time consuming. Your brother in Berlin feels as you do, that his creative spirit is being contained.

Why is it we know in our hearts that creativity is essential to growth and abundance, yet we choose to remain limited as individuals and societies? We fear our own creative selves. Most people choose the perception of safety and security (often accompanied by unhappiness) over adventure and bliss. The problem is—we buy into a paradigm that the safe lifestyle will always be there to support us. We pour our hearts and souls into products and processes outside of ourselves in hopes they will fill our financial cups and make us secure through all the days of our lives. Yet, you need only watch the news or read the headlines to see thousands of people displaced from their jobs every day due to circumstances beyond their control.

Life will always have elements outside our control, including nature's raging storms, economic crises, unexpected deaths of those we hold dear, and controversy at work and at home. Believing we can dictate the components of life is an illusion. But we *do* control how we react to the concerns and actions we choose to take.

Creativity will help us navigate rough waters and overcome perceived barriers. I use the word "perceived" with strong conviction, because a barrier for one person may seem like an opportunity to someone else. Perception is everything, and that's why I ask you to look at things more from a creative viewpoint.

What new, exquisite experience can you create from the materials and situations in your life?

Creativity is for everyone

People sometimes say creativity comes more naturally to those who are acquainted with struggle, strife, and even depression. Picture the starving artist whose greatest work appeared after a failed love affair; the musician, once a homeless youth reflecting back to sing poignant songs; or a writer whose bad experience in an office launched inspiration for a new book (insert wink here). I understand the point. Yes, tough stuff can be the fuel to light our fires, but I think of these situations as the *need for creativity* rising to address a problem. The creative part of us was always there, suited up and waiting to be called into the game from the bench. Could we have avoided or lessened some of those pitfalls if we allowed creativity to already be in play?

Resourcefulness, the act of using our inventiveness and ingenuity, is one aspect of being creative. When you have troubles to deal with, you start using your wits to solve the problem. Think back over the course of your life to some of the sticky situations you faced. Most of us aren't secret agents trying to diffuse a ticking bomb, but I imagine you can come up with a memory in which your cunning ability saved the day—for your child's favorite toy, a pet stranded in a tree, or the forgetful boss who misplaced a crucial report. Creativity is always within us, waiting for the opportunity to shine. Why not allow this part of ourselves to work effortlessly in our lives during every moment, not just times of dire need?

Creative passion at work

In a 2012 study of Chinese workers, researchers looked at creativity in generating innovative and practical ideas. They explored factors that stimulate employees to be creative while in the workplace, and then also investigated a motivational mechanism they define as "harmonious passion." The researchers assert that this form of passion is the "autonomous internalization of activities, making them part of one's identity, and thus creating a sense of personal enjoyment and free choice." They continue to report that harmonious passion is important to the Chinese for two key reasons. First, because China is working to transform its economy from manufacturing to innovation, which means changing the "made in China" approach to "invented in China." Creativity is essential for supporting this evolution. Second, China has welcomed the vision of constructing a more harmonious society overall for its people. The paper, published in the *Journal of Applied Psychology*[2], goes on to say that...

> "harmonious passion is implicit in the creative process. One reason is that harmonious passion enhances perceptions of autonomy and thus improves individual adaptivity and pro-activity in the creative process. The other reason is that harmonious passion generates the positive effect, excitement, and energy employees must have to connect divergent ideas, utilize broader resources, and experiment with original designs."

Wow! This is exciting. Research shows that having a strong sense of independence, support from those in higher positions, and the space to creatively express ourselves leads to greater innovation and productivity in the business environment.

This research also points to things we might logically suspect: when you're happy and engaged in your work you are more productive, efficient, and profitable for your employer. Allowing workers the breathing room to bring their best selves into the workplace will not only help morale, but also benefit the bottom line. Listen up managers and business owners—if you want to be on the leading edge of your industry, you will invite teams of talented employees to teach you a few things by harnessing their creativity and ingenuity. Release the fear of internal competition and create an environment in which you will all shine.

---

2   Dong Liu, Georgia Institute of Technology; Xiao-Ping Chen, University of Washington; and Xin Yao, University of Colorado, "From Autonomy to Creativity: A Multilevel Investigation of the Mediating Role of Harmonious Passion," Journal of Applied Psychology , 2011 (96): 294-309, http://dld.bz/dyCRF

> *"A business has to be involving, it has to be fun, and it has to exercise your creative instincts."*
> —Richard Branson

Years ago, one of my clients struggled at her job. She reported to a woman who was extremely smart and productive, and at first my client was excited about having such a prominent mentor. Her boss knew the business inside and out and would be the "go to" person for anything business related. Unfortunately, the boss was also insecure and a bit of a control freak who feared the talents of others and passive-aggressively undermined the strength of the team to advance her own interests and guard her position. While attempting to play team members against each other for information, she enticed them with promises of advancement they soon learned would never materialize. Threatened by change and the creativity of others, this person needed to be the boss and liked to remind her team they were mere minnows in her pond.

Her attitude was a big mistake for their small office. The bright group of workers could have become the best in the district if they were allowed to share their passions, ideas, experiences, and unique skills. One by one the staff left for other career opportunities, my client included. The manager staying behind to monitor the revolving door of new employees whose very existence threatened her. Perhaps if she allowed her team members the chance to creatively shine, she herself would discover new paths to greatness.

This little story isn't unique. These scenarios play out in business environments every day, in every town, in our country, and probably the rest of the world as well. Pop into a bank, restaurant, or insurance office next time you're on Main Street and be the fly on the wall for half an hour. You'll witness the drama of colliding egos. What are we to do about this? Are we condemned to work within a constant trap of fear and insecurity, letting the worst in ourselves bring out the worst in others?

To get a handle on a hectic work situation, we must start by taming the damn ego! Okay, before you get a bullwhip and head for your supervisor's house, know that I'm talking about *our* own egos and actions, not theirs. All change begins with self, and we will use our creative natures to get started on a positive path. This book is about how each of us can adopt new paradigms to create better environments. The companies we work for are made up of all of us, thus the changes need to begin right where we are. When we as individuals make beneficial shifts, our work atmosphere will shift for the better as well. This means by making positive shifts for ourselves, we will either improve our current job situations and be thrilled to stay working there, or we will manifest new opportunities to shine and be able to release what is not working in our lives.

To be seen and heard

The example of the fearful, control freak boss sheds light onto one of the biggest struggles workers face on the job—not being *seen* and valued as individuals. We spend most of our waking hours in service to our employers and innately yearn to be acknowledged, not only for our skills, but also for our sense of being—for our inner worth. This feeling of *not being seen* often leads to anxiety, fruitless competition between colleagues, production issues, and general displeasure in routine activities. It can give rise to a circle of insecurity where people constantly try to manipulate things to gain attention and favor from their directors—all in an effort to be seen. How did once happy new hires meld into neurotic, anxious, unhappy employees?

We often feel excited, optimistic, and downright wonderful when we're hired at a new job. That's because we're given the opportunity to share many aspects of who we are during job interviews. The employer shows interest in your education, experience, and background. Someone sits down with you, eye to eye, asking probing questions, making you feel special. The energy is similar to a first date, when two people project their best selves and try to make a great impression. These are moments when you feel seen and heard.

But once the actual job begins, focus on the individual self is often replaced by production demands, strict guidelines, and uncaring bosses. In too many workplaces you become just another worker bee, disillusioned and dissatisfied as *who you are* becomes less important than what you're expected to do. It's easy to fall into this role and give up.

Creativity takes courage

This is why creativity should be a crucial priority in all aspects of our lives—at work, at home, and in our spare time. It is our own responsibility to radiate our Light out to the world. You do not need permission to be yourself; simply have the courage to do it. Our creative natures are an expression of our selves and the way we share our spark with the world. It is essential for each of us to foster a lifestyle where we can bring ourselves fully to whatever we do every day, including our professions. When we do, we feel more secure and perform better at our duties, because we're comfortable in our own skin and able to simply "be" and do.

> *"Creativity takes courage."*
> —Henri Matisse

I know some of you are saying, "Yeah, Deb, I get that, but I don't have the sort of job that leaves room for me to be me."

Actually, you do. You may not see the opportunity from your present perspective, so I need you to try and see it creatively with me right now. Even workers such as police officers, nurses, and industrial employees who must wear uniforms have the opportunity to express their creativity in subtle ways. Whether it's a hairstyle, a small piece of jewelry or the design of your socks and undies, there are limitless creative ways you can express who you are and foster a greater creative environment for yourself. Once you open the door to creativity, there's no stopping it.

For many years my husband, Mark, went to his manufacturing job carrying a lunch box covered with colorful stickers and signs expressing his various likes and opinions. An ever-evolving collage of words, pictures, and smarmy sayings, the box became a comical talking point at lunchtime with his friends and co-workers. Although he wore a basic uniform and steel-toed boots for safety, his quirky creation allowed him freedom of expression in an environment that had little room for such things. Much like a student who decorates book covers at school, he found a way to let his Self shine through. Mark has always been a creative guy, often wearing a kilt instead of pants on his days off as he wanders our small town with his camera, taking photographs of scenery and antique homes. An eccentric before old age, he has the courage to live freely and express himself.

Free expression in accessories and clothing isn't just for you and me. Our 41st President of the United States of America, George H.W. Bush, is known to wear wild and colorful socks with his conservative gentleman's attire to speeches, meetings, and public events. This is a small facet of who he is and lets us know a little more about him and see his soul shining through. We can relate to each other more when we allow our eyes to truly see.

Don't squeeze yourself into a box

It's important not to compartmentalize your life by turning into a different version of yourself for each environment you're in. I'll get more into this during our next chapter on authenticity. Realize at this moment, your employer got a glimpse of your inner spark the day you were hired. They recognize it's in there and are actually relying on that part of you to take their company forward with your vast ideas and brilliant innovations.

You are the only *you* in the world, so make the most of it and accept fully all aspects of yourself. Don't set limitations for yourself for fear of looking bad or making a mistake. Don't be afraid to fail. Let's finally allow our inner eleven-year-old art student to mix mediums and design a life with wild abandon. Who knows—your boss might like to see you in wacky orange striped socks or a vintage paisley tie.

The amazing thing about creativity is that it will take whatever form you choose. Being creative is shapeless, colorless, no odor, without matter, weight or size ... until you determine the form you wish it to take.

You have superpowers

Your creativity is your very own super power, with the ability to instantly transform into whatever you wish. We can bring fun and exuberance into our lives, helping us cope with the parts that are not always enjoyable. If things need to be done anyway, why not find a creative and light-hearted way to do them? Life is already heavy, but we have the power within us to lighten the load.

Those of you with a more analytical nature may not see yourselves as artists or feel comfortable diving into a palette of paint. Rest easy, you still have creative juices flowing through you. Remember, creativity takes many shapes and shows in our ability to troubleshoot problems, deal with customers and clients, write computer code, invent new methods, and even wrangle feisty children. You should find the expression that's comfortable for you.

My friend, artist David Goldstein, co-authored a book entitled *Creative You*,[3] which utilizes your personality type to help discover your creativity type. If you like the thought of exploring creativity through a psychological model, I suggest you wade right into his book, which is filled with excellent information and techniques.

Barriers and bridges

Throughout our lives, we all face barriers that block our progress and stifle our creative urges. We also find—and build—bridges that help us overcome obstacles and arrive safely at our destinations. Though these barriers and bridges to creativity are unique for everyone, they do have similarities. In the next section I identify both positive and negative things you may encounter during your creative journey. Tested by my clients, these ideas can either extinguish or ignite your inner fires.

---

3   David Goldstein and Otto Kroeger. *Creative You*. New York: Atria Books/Beyond Words, 2013.

Keep these suggestions in heart and mind as you stoke the flames of creativity in your life and begin to ignite CALM.

Ignite Creativity

Don't stay in your comfort zone: This is a nice way of being stuck in a rut! Yes, it's cozy to feel safe and warm in the same space all the time, but realize if we eat the same foods, see only the same group of friends, and listen to only one musical group, we are eliminating other possibilities and hindering our growth. You won't even know what else is out there. This type of behavior at work can limit career advancement, because you may be perceived as rigid and even lazy.

Avoid electronic immersion: This is a chronic problem in our society. You'll see people from all walks of life completely focused on a laptop, smart phone, or television screen while ignoring the natural beauty and dynamic experiences around them. When we're captivated by the artificial reality designed by others, we close ourselves off from things that awaken our inner artist. We lose touch with the people, events, and experiences that form the palette of our lives.

Don't always follow the leader: It is nice to have strong people leading the way in our professional environment and our communities. But if we only follow others, we're limited by their set of rules, judgments, and opinions, denying ourselves the chance to excel in areas we never thought possible. If you can't be distinguished from the crowd, how will anyone ever learn about what you have to offer?

Don't let fear reign: Fear of failing and looking the fool is one of the biggest roadblocks to creativity and a life fully lived. Allowing fear to hold you in its grip guarantees you'll remain right where you are, with little opportunity for success and advancement. No one *but you* can make a true change in how you live your life. Would you be reading this if you were 100 percent happy with how things are going?

Don't overvalue money and things: The illusion that money and things can buy happiness has been with us since the beginning of time. No matter how many people tell us this isn't so, we laugh and say, "Well, I'd like to try that for myself!" Addictions to money, possessions, fame, and accolades keep us trapped in a continuous cycle of wanting more for doing less. This colors our perception of what's valuable in our world, leading us to disregard the power and beauty all around us.

Don't undervalue time: We often think we'll have plenty of time to do things *later*. I'll take that adventure, apply for my dream job, and spend more time with my children when I don't have to work late, or when I get caught up with things. It is a sobering realization that we have less than 1000 weekends to share with our families while our children are growing up, and less than 4000 weekends in an entire lifetime to age 75. The ability to value each moment and be creative with our time may be the best gift the Universe can give us.

Be a citizen of the world: Nothing helps creative energy flow like immersing ourselves in a new and different way of living. Seeing how people work, play, and relate to one another in communities and countries unknown to us will open our minds to innovation and our hearts to understanding. The passion and purposes of others can spark our own introspection and inspire us to view ourselves as citizens of the world. You can do this without traveling far from home. Find a creative way to reach out to other cultures.

Play well with others: Collaborating on creative pursuits and projects on the job gives us amazing potential to expand ourselves, often challenging us to step beyond perceived limitations. As Aristotle taught, "the whole is more than the sum of its parts." The synergy of a group is more powerful than individuals acting alone. Open yourself to the teachers around you and your own ability to share knowledge.

Role reversal: What better way to mix it up than by trying out a new role? Trading places in the workplace, even for a day, is an effective technique to give us increased understanding of procedures and greater empathy for the challenges other people face. This is also a powerful practice in our private lives, within the diverse perspectives and responsibilities of our family and friends.

Just say yes: Try saying "yes" instead of "no" to invitations you receive. The Universe provides us with unlimited opportunities to expand ourselves and live creatively. We often disregard a call to action because we're too fearful or tired to try something new. Step out of your shell and reach for the challenge. Maybe the person who invited you sees a spark in your eyes and recognizes your potential for greatness.

Try on a new style: This is one of the easiest ways to, in this very moment, make a positive creative shift in your life. Whether you change the clothes you wear, the way you speak, or the food you eat, making a change can be fun and add energy to a life that feels a bit humdrum. You need not abandon what you love; simply spice things up with new color choices, friendships, or hobbies. Trust me, you won't regret it!

Invite adventure: At the end of our days, we aren't going to look back and wish we'd spent more time feeling bored. That bored feeling at work or home is a sign you aren't challenging yourself enough in life. Only you have the power to change this. Know when its time to leave the computers to their own devices and create a life that pleases your sense of exploration. You needn't be rich to strut out the back door and see what exciting things are happening right around the block.

Ignition points

- Look at the most colorful characters in your life; the artists, the writers, and the quirky inventor down the street. What do you admire most about them? Realize what you see in them is also a reflection of yourself.

- Step outside your comfort zone and do something artistic and different. If you normally prefer ballet, mix it up and go to a rock concert. If you like to draw, take a pottery or cooking class instead. Allow your creativity to find alternate routes.

Chapter Two Exercise – Ignite CALM

What do you see in others?

In this exercise, I'd like you to select five people in your life to reflect on. You will complete five statements about each of them. The five people must include the following: a supervisor, a colleague, a romantic partner, a parent or mentor of yours, and a child—either your own or one you're familiar with. Each person must be someone you now know or have known well in the past. You'll make it too difficult if you attempt to do this with an acquaintance or stranger.

Begin by creating a column for each person, writing their names or initials on a sheet of paper, leaving room to respond below. Next, complete the statements for each person by writing your answers below their respective names. The five statements are:

1. I admire how this person_____
2. I dislike how this person_____
3. I consider this person's best trait to be _____
4. I believe this person could teach me most about _____
5. If I had to choose a crayon to describe his or her personality, it would be the color _____

Congratulations on flexing your creative muscles by doing the exercise! As you can see, it's a bit unconventional. However this exercise is essential to help you see how you look at things. Look over the chart you created based on relationships in your life. Are your responses mostly positive or negative? Are they humorous or harsh?

Did you tell the truth or were you fibbing to be polite in case someone found the page?

When doing any of the exercises you should have full freedom to explore in honesty, so if you're concerned about confidentiality, use initials or your own code. This is your work and you need to be comfortable with it and understand what you're exploring.

Examine your responses and see how you described yourself. Yes, yourself! Every relationship in our lives provides an opportunity to see facets of ourselves. This isn't good or bad; it simply is. If you stated your lover's best trait is compassion and warmth, realize that's also one of your best traits. Whether you recognize it or not, this trait is within you and of value to you. The same can be said for disliking your boss's temper. That trait may reflect issues you have yet to process about your life experiences with anger and rage.

Relationships and how we see them are spectacular opportunities to learn more about our own natures and how we walk in this world. What you see in others is alive within you. Each of us gets to decide which of these traits we want to celebrate or tame.

Chapter Three
Authenticity

"Hard times arouse an instinctive desire for authenticity."
—Coco Chanel

THE SECOND COMPONENT in our CALM approach is authenticity, which means being genuine and real in how we live our lives. In a culture bombarded with the fake and contrived, being authentic has become a rare commodity. Embracing authenticity in your life means allowing your spirit to lead the way without giving in to pressure and projection from others. And the best part is, you get to be open and honest with others. People will respect this. Your family, friends, and colleagues like knowing where they stand with you, because you mean what you say and you do what you say you'll do.

In the workplace, you may face situations that threaten the authentic self. As you know by now, my corporate job did not allow me to give care and attention to others. Compassion wasn't part of the company's business model and they perceived my actions as rebellion. I had the option to change who I was and what I was doing, but that threatened my personal prime directive: being of service to others holistically, in body, mind, and spirit. When something goes against your soul's mission, it's impossible for the relationship to continue without causing great damage to everyone involved. This is true for all connections, in our jobs, marriages, families, and other relationships.

What is authenticity?

This concept goes beyond style and personal appearance; it's about being true to YOU and fully processing and owning your experiences without concern for what other people think. I see authenticity as a way of being, an aura exuded from every pore of your body in which you are open in both your strength and your frailty. Your "misses" are as essential and important as your "hits," because you savor the bitter along with the sweet.

My friend, best-selling author and self-development expert Lisa McCourt, embraces "radical authenticity" in her book *Juicy Joy*[4], teaching readers how to live the sweet, juicy life of freedom by fully accepting who we are. Her lifestyle and career are the best demonstration of how it works, blissfully. Everyone who meets Lisa can attest to her vibrant spirit, generosity, and pure sweetness of heart. We need more people like Lisa in this world: positive and upbeat, brave and successful in her authenticity.

We live in a time when people are preoccupied by how they look on the outside. The *American Academy of Facial Plastic and Reconstructive Surgery* reports that plastic surgery is on the rise in our country because of the preoccupation with "selfies," the self-portrait photographs we take with smart phones and post on social networking sites. Apparently, many people are unhappy about how they look from these contrived angles and are opting to go under the knife to correct their flaws. The increase in "selfie surgery" was revealed in the Academy's recent analysis of its members—an annual poll of the organization's 2,700 members to uncover recent developments in facial plastic surgery. One in three facial plastic surgeons they surveyed saw an increase in requests for procedures due to "patients being more self-aware of looks in social media." The

---

[4] Lisa McCort, *Juicy Joy: 7 Simple Steps to Your Glorious, Gutsy Self,* Hay House, March 20, 2012).

members examined reported a ten percent increase in rhinoplasty (nose jobs) over the previous year, a six percent rise in eyelid procedures, and a seven percent increase in hair transplants. The study showed that plastic surgery procedures are increasing among those under the age of 30.

Of course it's okay to have plastic surgery if that's what you want. We all have the right to do what we wish with our lives and our bodies. I get my hair colored, have a tattoo, and had work done on my smile and nose after several fractures and chronic breathing issues. The ironic thing is, my nose was fractured again when I was accidentally struck by my daughter's knee, so the slight crook I have now is authentically mine.

I do find it troubling that, as a society, we're vain and obsessed with physical appearances and judge ourselves too harshly. Perhaps it's time to move past the physical and take a look at our inner lives. We must expand our definition of beauty and re-examine our priorities. It's possible to fall in love with your laugh-line wrinkles and crooked nose. If you think about it, we would never judge a close friend or loved one the harsh way we judge ourselves. Embracing all aspects of who we are, authentically, is the transcendental shift we need as individuals and as a society.

My friends, Raji Kelley Simpson and her husband, Jeffrey Simpson have created a virtual course titled "Selfie Love" in which they encourage students to explore self portraits as "an act of radical self love, expression, and freedom." Jeffrey, a longtime photographer and instructor in the new field of "iPhoneography," brings his artistic talents and vast technical knowledge to the students, while Raji, a teacher of yoga and spirituality, brings her own dynamism to the class and encourages their students to heal and see themselves in new ways. She says, "I took my first self-portrait on the day I was diagnosed with a disEASE. The image is one of my first images that offered me a whole new way to be the witness; I could see exactly where I was, and simultaneously the artist; that could create and see myself in a future that I desired, feeling how I want to feel. I infused hundreds of images with thoughts of radical self-love, creative expression, and freedom. The effects were nothing short of miraculous." Their innovative work takes a challenging, often destructive, habit and recreates it into a compelling tool of transformation. Bravo!

> *"Truth is a point of view, but authenticity can't be faked."*
> —Peter Guber

Authenticity on the Job

When I refer to authenticity in the workplace, I don't mean oversharing your personal life by constantly telling stories about your childhood, discussing your feelings about everything that happens, or bringing your personal beliefs into every discussion. Authenticity means you live your life according to your own values and goals, rather than those of other people.

At all times, you are true to your own personality, values, and spirit. You take responsibility for your mistakes. Your actions align with your values. You're honest with yourself and others (but not brutally honest). This means you come across as a genuine person, even if you have to go against the crowd and possibly miss opportunities for advancement.

Does being authentic in life truly lead to greater happiness at work? Yes, it does. When you're in alignment with your true self, you are consciously creating your opportunities. If you go against the grain of your own belief system, either by choice or force, your world contracts and it becomes difficult to see beyond your own pain and frustration.

The key is to stop the madness of trying to do things that are not part of your value system. The benefits of authenticity include:

- ◆ Dealing with problems: When you're honest with yourself and the people around you, you'll feel stronger and more confident. Problems will seem less daunting.
- ◆ Meeting your potential: When you follow your own values, you'll feel more satisfied with what you achieve in life, knowing you've taken control and gone after what's best for you.

- Self-esteem and confidence: Trusting yourself to make the right decisions leads to higher self-esteem, which will in turn boost your self-confidence.
- Lower stress levels: What could be more stressful than pretending to be someone else all day long? Behaving in accordance with your own values and Self brings happiness and self-respect.
- Integrity: When who you are, what you do, and the things you believe in line up, you've achieved integrity. This is something the people around you will see and respect, even when they don't agree with you.
- Respect and trust from others: Do you respect people you know who are true to themselves? Do you trust them to do the right thing? You can be one of those people.

Let's not be judgmental. A job that doesn't resonate with you may be perfect for someone else. At the insurance company where I worked, many people relished their jobs and were extremely successful. Good for them! I know a man who loves regulations and statistical research. When he speaks about his projects he is passionate and alive, his eyes flashing and speech rapid. Most of the subject matter goes right over my head, and between you and me, I find his occupation of never ending numbers to be incredibly boring and complicated. But his energy and excitement are palpable—I know he's happy in his work and his life. Each profession can be a special "calling" for the people who love their jobs. The secret is—don't force yourself into a mold that doesn't fit your authentic self.

What does it mean to be at your best at work? Okay, let's call ourselves on this right now. Our best is being engaged, active, open, honest, and striving to work together to achieve goals and celebrate mutual success. It is NOT being lazy, passing the buck, complaining, blaming, and avoiding responsibility for our own actions. As I have said a few times and in a few different ways, this is your life to create. The responsibility and freedoms are yours for the taking. If you cannot see yourself as the creator of your own life and remain trapped in a victim mentality, you will be stuck in the mire and the muck of discontent in your profession—and in other aspects of your life.

Even though challenges and struggles will exist, and we realize they will, this is all a part of living a colorful, authentic life. I'm not talking about creating drama around every corner; in fact, the opposite. When we take things as they come using the best of ourselves to navigate the situation, life is less dramatic and more rewarding. We see the significance of circumstances without getting caught up in an ego-dripped spectacle. If you work in a job with drama queens, try to stand back and let theatrics pass around you. *Be the eye of the storm.* If that isn't possible and you find yourself continually upset at work, the time may be ripe for a change.

Authenticity and happiness

In his blog for *Psychology Today*,[5] Rom Brafman discusses the link between authenticity and happiness from his perspective as a humanistic psychologist. He believes authenticity is a "huge factor in the process of healing," because happiness and an overall sense of well-being increase when people find their authentic selves.

I think he's right. When we strip away the challenges to our authentic nature, we feel free and more open to the possibilities of the Universe. When we participate in activities that don't fit us, we can become lethargic, moody, and downright depressed. Picture caging a beautiful, wild animal; the animal withdraws, stops eating, and may even die of a broken heart, a shattered spirit. Our professions should not cage our spirits! Strive to be in your element, where all things come together in a bright display of skill and talent. We must seek to create experiences and opportunities that ignite our inner fire and stimulate our active, curious minds.

---

5 Rom Brafman, PhD, "Authenticity and Happiness: A Real Link, Don't Be Swayed," August 18, 2008.
http://dld.bz/dyCRQ

This belief is supported by a recent academic paper written by Cable et al.[6] The researchers, who hail from the campuses of London Business School, Harvard University, and The University of North Carolina, propose an alternative way of viewing organizational socialization to address the primary needs of both the businesses and employees. Drawing on past authenticity research, they suggest "organizational socialization is optimized when organizations start by recognizing and highlighting newcomers' best selves at the very beginning of the employment relationship, when identity negotiation is a critical concern for both parties."

Their research indicates an individual's best self emerges from utilizing and being recognized for their "signature strengths," which enhances workers' feelings of authenticity.

What are your signature strengths? Does your job use these strengths, or are they ignored? Even worse, are your strengths a burden in your present position?

Research tells us authenticity is a critical component for the success of both businesses and their employees. Many employers do not recognize this, but you know it's true. If we go against our authentic selves, we often pay a price with our happiness and health. When we begin feeling depleted and worn by the pressures of daily living that's a sign we are not in balance with our true selves and need to make a change. Something is out of place somewhere and needs to be addressed. It is crucial to look at our lives holistically: physically, mentally, emotionally, and spiritually to ensure we're firing on all cylinders.

Years of neglect and poor habits will take a toll on us. Healing is a process, not a snap of the fingers, and may take time to integrate into our lives. Give yourself that time and attention. Speak with a health professional you respect about your state of wellness and develop a plan to bring yourself to an optimal place. We are all

---

6 Dan Cable, Francesca Gino, and Brad Staats, "Breaking Them In or Revealing Their Best? Reframing Socialization around Newcomer Self-Expression," *Working Papers, February 17, 2012a*, http://hbswk.hbs.edu/item/6954.html

unique and being well can take many forms. Although my daughter is profoundly disabled, she knows wellness and peace. Her medical challenges are a part of who she is, not *all* of who she is. When we deal with life authentically, as it comes, we can all be grateful for a sense of wellbeing.

> *"We need to find the courage to say no to the things and people that are not serving us if we want to rediscover ourselves and live our lives with authenticity."*
> —Barbara de Angelis

Adventures in authenticity

An interesting opportunity came to me after my departure from the corporate world. A few weeks after I left the cubicle, while writing this book, I received a message from a friend who publishes a holistic journal with distribution across numerous states. I had written for this beautiful, heart-centered publication in the past and also advertised my charity's events and services there. Our email exchange was friendly as we caught up with each other on the happenings of life. She was on her way back to wellness after a tough battle with cancer that required months of hospitalization and nearly took her life. "My heart breaks that I never found someone to care for the journal," she said. Keeping the publication going was more than she wanted to do at this point in time and her soul ached when she thought about the conscious collaboration of the talented writers, teachers, and healers that would be silenced.

"I'm sorry, I never thought to ask how much you were selling the journal for," I replied. Knowing hundreds of professionals in the mind-body-spirit genre, I imagined one of them would have funds available to become a publisher of a holistic magazine, especially a journal established for over 14 years with an impressive multi-state circulation. She explained to me she wasn't looking to sell. Rather, she and her partner, were looking for someone who could hold its space and light. Our email exchange went on for days as we followed the energy of the situation and talked about potentials. I then traveled to meet with them in person and explore what the role of "caretaker" meant.

After a meeting of hearts and minds, they decided to explore options to donate their publication, *Inner Tapestry*[7], to the holistic charity I had founded several years before, *The HeartGlow Center*. Plans are now underway to accept this gift and for the publication to become a digital magazine and holistic directory published by the charity. We will continue sharing the wisdom and education of talented holistic practitioners, now on a global scale, and will include other teachers I've met over the years in my travels. All proceeds from ad sponsorships and listings will support the charity's mission and programs. This is conscious collaboration at its highest!

This unique opportunity wasn't something I went looking for, but when viewed from a higher perspective it's easy to see how the Universe worked with me to create an opportunity in alignment with my soul. I had defined my personal prime directive as *being of service to others holistically, body, mind, and spirit*. What better way to do this than being the editor of a holistic magazine in which I will collaborate with people I respect and admire to make the world a better place? And doing so in service to the charity I hold in my heart is the icing on the cake with a side of chocolate ice cream!

This publication will not only sustain itself, but also fund The HeartGlow Center's other charitable programs, which provide support for people who are facing life's diverse challenges, such as coping after loss of a loved one or living with chronic illness and disability. I could never have dreamed something so grand ... it's a good thing the Universe could.

Staying true to myself in good times and bad allowed this to come to fruition. This is a fabulous example of how, when we live in authenticity, we have unlimited potential and open the door to all possibilities. *What incredible adventure will you create when you also live authentically?*

---

7   *Inner Tapestry Magazine*, http://www.innertapestry.org/

When we think of adventurous business people it doesn't take long for the name Sir Richard Branson to come to mind. The English founder of Virgin Group, which is comprised of more than 400 companies, Branson is well-known to be his own man. A maverick. A billionaire. A risk-taker. A humanitarian. Traveling the world in every form and fashion from hot air balloon to high-speed boat, Sir Richard is a prime example of someone who lives an authentic lifestyle. His courageous ventures have made and cost him millions. His escapades often spark ridicule and distain from people in more conservative schools of thought. Personally, I adore his energy and zest for life.

Many folks mistakenly think Richard Branson's vast financial riches give him the freedom to be authentic. In truth, if you read his background, you will find his entrepreneurial zest began during his teenage years and he created that wealth by following his passions. His authenticity helps manifest the abundance and success we now see in his life. Richard Branson often says "yes" to life. We all have a choice in deciding how to look at situations and what actions to take. The beautifully creative world is patiently awaiting our responses and level of engagement.

In your life, do you often say *no* or *yes*?

In my life, the generous donation of the holistic journal was available for others to act on, as the giver had been seeking a caretaker for months. Did others allow this opportunity to slip through their fingers because they viewed it as a burden instead of a blessing? Did their words or energy say "no?" We may never know for sure, but I'm grateful my organization was in proper vibration and timing to receive such a gift—to say "yes" as though standing on a mountaintop with arms open wide.

As with creativity, we can take certain steps to bring authenticity into our lives, at home, on the job, and in everything we do. Like making a campfire, you need the right components coming together at the right time: a safe spot, fuel to burn, a spark to ignite it all, and airflow to keep it going. I love watching Les Strout of the cable TV show "Survivorman" gather his materials and make do with the limited resources he has on hand in a secluded and sometimes hostile environment. In most cases, with intelligence, experience, and ingenuity, he gets that fire going—and we can too!

Below are my suggested things—the "Do's and Don't's" for building your inner campfire. S'mores are optional, but highly recommended. I will start with the "don'ts" intentionally, because it's more powerful and positive to finish up with what we should do. Keep these tips in mind and heart as you add fuel to the flames of authenticity in your life and begin to ignite CALM.

Ignite Authenticity

Don't fall for facades: It's time we realize that much of what we see in the traditional media and on television is fake and should not be emulated. These people are in exaggerated situations acting in a manner that will gain attention, either negative or positive. They don't seem to care as long as it's attention. Don't buy into the drama and spectacle, because it's all illusion. Look past the flash to find the soul.

Don't hide your skills: I've seen it time and time again with clients. Beautiful, talented people hide their own skills to prevent conflict. Do not allow yourself to be bullied by arrogant people on the job, at school, or at home. Manipulators deal in fear, but you don't need to buy into it or change YOU for them. Shine on. And while you're at it, post for that higher position—maybe it's time for you to be the boss.

Don't carry around old baggage: We all wear the scars of tough experiences from the past, whether they arise from bad jobs, controlling parents, traumatic events, or tough relationships. Life has messy moments, no doubt about it. Now simply put the baggage down. Honor the wisdom garnered from your past experiences and then release it forever. Move into a new tomorrow with a lighter load. You'll discover a more authentic you when you shake the ghosts from your luggage and silence the disapproving voices.

Don't be a pleaser: People pleasers can certainly be nice, but are they happy? Always yielding to the preferences and opinions of others clogs your own natural flow and can build resentment within relationships. Get along with others, but do so while also honoring your own truth and voice. Things usually work out better in the end when each party is true to themselves. The people we respect and love deserve our authenticity ... and so do we.

Don't lie to fit in: This might sound like something you witness in a schoolyard, but it takes place in every worksite known to humankind. We lie in an attempt to bond with others and be successful. Our society even glamorizes such behavior by saying, "fake it until you make it," as if that's some sort of motivational tool. Be yourself and enjoy each moment at whatever skill level you're in. It is what it is, until it isn't. Love the truth of who you are!

Don't trap your frustrations: Many of us were raised to be quiet and not give voice to our feelings. We learn to snuff out our fire and dampen our unique views of the world around us. Although some people view this as being polite, it can catch up with you and lead to hostility, rage, and health issues, because those pent up frustrations are trapped in your body and energy field. Learn to express your opinions, emotions, and feelings in a safe and professional manner.

Be honest with yourself: There comes a time when we realize we're responsible for all aspects of our lives. No one else to blame or honor; it's all on us. We must accept the Self fully with integrity, authenticity, and brutal honesty. If we fool ourselves about our behavior, addictions, and circumstances, who are we actually benefiting? No one. Love yourself enough to respect the truth, and accept without question that you can handle it.

Embrace personal freedom: You don't need a leather jacket, motorcycle, and the open road to find freedom—although that sounds like great fun. Create opportunities to be alone and do exactly what you want. Most of us don't leave adequate down time, and when we do have it, we sleep from exhaustion. Put on your favorite music, rent your dream car, and go for a long drive. Or simply take time to journal, go fishing, or paint. This is your freedom to enjoy, so use it! You'll find you're much happier at work when you create happiness in your off hours.

Make room to grow: Think of yourself as a gorgeous, growing plant stuck in a tiny pot. It's time to make room so your curious roots can find more sustenance and secure your foundation. We all need space to expand our roots and bloom, baby, bloom! Change your environment; sign on for a new project, and look at opportunities in uncharted areas. Challenge yourself to think bigger and take on more responsibility. Dissatisfaction at work often comes from boredom and not having the opportunity to expand.

Eliminate toxic connections: Easy to say, but often difficult to do. We must value ourselves highly to stop being poisoned by those around us. Our health, happiness, and general sense of wellbeing is our own responsibility and cannot be left to the whims of someone who could care less. Their actions and energy usually show their true motives. Take the signs from the Universe and let them go. If a co-worker or supervisor is toxic, be clear and honest about your concerns. You might help your company by being the authentic one who calls this person on the rubbish they're creating.

Plan a trip: Where in the world do you dream of going? If money, time, and distance posed no obstacle, what destination would you choose to explore for a month? Now that you have your location picked out, make it so. In this very moment, start a change jar to save money. Order a destination-guide to study the locale, or pick out the special scarf you'll wear on the plane. It doesn't matter if months, years, or even decades pass before you actually make the trip. What counts is taking steps every day to make your authentic dream a reality.

Clean house: You can take this both literally and figuratively; time to clean up the clutter in all corners of your world. Shift the energy in your space by eliminating objects that no longer resonate with you. Replace what you discarded with items you adore. Pass along ancient treasures that make you cringe to someone who will enjoy them. Add your own personal zest to your home, office, and vehicle with artistic or fun items. Allowing people to see reflections of your authentic nature in the places you spend time is comforting and increases productivity.

Ignition points

- Think back to your favorite age. How old were you? Why was it a favorite time of your life so far? Bring something from that time and space into your life again. Whether it is a beloved song, classic book, or something delicious to eat, welcome that energy to your heart again.
- Find space and time to be ALONE. Out loud and with deep authentic sincerity, say the things you've always wanted to say and never voiced before. Allow the pent up expressions to get out. Whether it's a declaration of love, anger, or even a simple hello to a cute stranger, visualize the situation and say it loud and proud. You can use a stuffed animal as a receiving partner, if it will help you. They always understand.

Chapter Three Exercise – Ignite CALM

Who are you?

In this exercise, I would like you to go on a deep exploration of what it means to be *you*.

- What do you like?
- What don't you like?
- How do you see yourself in this world?

We're going to approach this in a fun, whimsical way to take the pressure off. There are no right or wrong answers, simply your answers to your questions. I hope you will gain insight on your life and see areas that may need more time and attention. This is to aid your evolution and growth and help you feel comfortable in your own authentic nature. Whether you're a stoic person, conservative, a wild one, an academic—or all those things at the same time, it doesn't matter. The important thing is to recognize who you are, authentically.

Let's get started. On a scale of 1 to 10, rate how the following statements resonate with you. The number 1 and numbers on the lower end of the scale represent "no" and less resonance, while the higher numbers closer 10 are "yes" and more in resonance. If I read the question, "Do you love cats?" my answer would be 10, because I'm a lifelong cat lover. Others people may be on the other end of the scale if they dislike cats, or somewhere in between.

Please rate your responses to the following ten statements:
1. I am addicted to my job. I never seem to stop working.
2. I love what I do for a living.
3. I would consider myself a giver.
4. I am bored most of the time, I can't find anything that piques my interest.
5. I spend more than 12 hours a day on an electronic device, such a computer or smart phone.
6. I love being out in nature and spend significant time outdoors.
7. I take plenty of alone time for myself.
8. I have no fear about being myself in every part of my life.
9. I easily get jealous of people in my life for what they have.
10. Overall, I consider my life to be a happy one.

How did you do? How does it feel? Now that you've ranked the statements, I want you to take a closer look. Did you have many extremes with numerous 1's and 10's, or were most of your answers somewhere in the middle? Did you favor a ranking and assign the same number to most of the statements? Do you feel you were honest in your answers?

Each question on its own can offer insight into how you perceive that aspect of your life. Collectively, the questions can show balance, or lack of it, in your life. For example, if you ranked a 10, "Yes, I am always on an electronic device" and at the same time you don't get time alone or out in nature ... perhaps more time enjoying the natural world may be in order. You can decide for yourself.

I ask you to continue posing questions of yourself as you move through each day. What is your interest level for different activities? Slowly, you will start to see your special desires and interests moving to the forefront in your life. The expectations and projections of others will no longer have staying power when you tune into your authentic self and create the life you truly desire to live.

Chapter Four
Luminosity

> *"The dancer's body is simply the luminous manifestation of the soul."*
> -Isadora Duncan

THE THIRD COMPONENT in our CALM approach is luminosity, your radiance and the ability to shine your Light. At this point you may be saying, "What is she talking about?" Most of us never consider "being a beacon" as a priority in our professional lives. Applications for employment don't usually include "glowing, shining, and gleaming."

However, we do describe people in the workplace as "bright," meaning they're smart, confident, and have it all together. We also refer to our wise elders as "luminaries," or leaders in their fields who light the way for others. We describe our personalities as having a light side, which embodies positive traits and a dark side with more negative traits. We seem to naturally recognize a source of light within us. Even at summer camp we sang, "This little light of mine, I'm going to let it shine!"

Luminosity means celebrating the Light of your soul, when you radiate and demonstrate the best of who you are. If this idea is beyond your normal comfort zone, please bear with me and allow yourself to step into the glow for a while. I'm not referring to a specific religion or a particular system. I'm discussing the spirit within you; your essence. You may view this light as part of your soul, or–if you aren't comfortable with religious views–reframe it as personality, psyche, mind, or a character trait. We are talking about the *spark* within you, beyond your body, that makes you uniquely who you are.

Lovely, luminous people already surround you in life. You may recognize luminosity in a favorite teacher, pastor, medical professional, coach, or even the young kid who bags your groceries. We've all met people who radiate light. Purely put, radiance attracts. We don't always realize why we're drawn to the Light of another, but we are attracted. Magnetism and grace captivate us and pull us closer to the warm glow. Many people in the public eye have a strong internal light and proudly show it. This is often why they achieve success and acclaim in their professions.

Performers share their souls with us, expressed through dance, song, or prose. We connect with them heart-to-heart and feel transformed by their sincere giving. Think of how easy it is to have a crush on a celebrity or a musician. They sparkle and we get starry eyed. We see and feel their Light. A person of Light moves us, connecting through feelings and emotion. Others may try to fake it, blinding us with spotlights, glitter, and glam in hopes we won't be able to tell the difference. But we yearn to see the true light within, not a cheap imitation. Look for the sparkle in their eyes, the Light of the soul.

Each of us enters this world with a soul glowing within us, and we can learn to intensify that brilliance. While some people seem to naturally shine from first breath, others are more subtle in their vibrancy. As we grow older, many of us attempt to hide our Light, fearing we won't like the "real" person.

We call our daughter Raegan a "Rae of sunshine" because her joyful spirit showers everyone around her with bright love. Although physically and medically disabled, she excels in the shining department. Raegan doesn't have an ego mind, fear, control issues, or day-to-day worries to block her Light. She simply *is*, which allows her pure soul to glow.

Being luminous means proudly sharing the light of your soul, the goodness inside you. Each of us, no matter what our profession or background, can live an illuminating life and positively affect others by being kind, generous, and loving. I have met radiating soldiers, nurses, and auto mechanics. Your profession doesn't matter: the key is *how* you go about doing something. Our attitudes, actions, and how we live our lives dictate the shine factor. As the adage says, "you can choose to radiate or to drain." Are you going to make the world a better place by shining as only you can, or will you spend your time and energy complaining about life? Most of us fall somewhere in between, depending on the day we're having.

Light blockers

In our fast-paced, competitive society, we tend to get in our own way by constructing light blockers in the form of fear, frustration, projection, limitations, and judgments.

- We **fear** to reveal ourselves because people may not respond the way we want. Conditioned to value others first, we diminish our own radiance.
- We're **frustrated** when things don't go our way, so we try to change who we are or force shifts on the people in our lives.
- We **project** ideas about what might happen onto daily situations, which leads to unneeded fear and worry.
- **Limitations** can be stepping stones, but not if we turn them into roadblocks. Our capacity to transcend is greater than we think.
- **Judging** ourselves, others, and situations harshly leads to negative feelings that dim the Light. Aim for observation and understanding.

Too often we think we aren't good enough in this world. We want to wait until we're wildly successful and everyone loves us. THEN, we can safely shine our Light. Until that day we try to guess what people want, and then we attempt to morph into that projection so we can make everyone happy. Ugh! Wouldn't you rather be like Raegan, and simply shine?

Are we capable of taking down the blinds we've hung over the windows of our souls? Yes, we are! The Center for Compassion and Altruism Research and Education (CCARE) [8] at the Stanford School of Medicine was founded in 2008 with "the explicit goal of promoting, supporting, and conducting rigorous scientific studies of compassion and altruistic behavior." *CCARE*, under the direction of Dr. James Doty, Clinical Professor of Neurosurgery, has worked in partnership with a number of leading neuroscientists, behavioral scientists, geneticists, and biomedical researchers to "closely examine the physiological and psychological correlates of compassion and altruism." While medical science overall has made significant gains in treating diseases of the mind, significantly fewer explorations have been pursued to look at the positive qualities of the mind including empathy, altruism, and compassion. *CCARE* believes these traits "are innate to us and lie at the very centerpiece of our common humanity. Our capacity to feel compassion has ensured the survival and thriving of our species over millennia." What an exciting time to be living, we are starting to officially make the connection that being a beacon in our world is a benefit to not only ourselves but also to the world as a whole.

Illuminating people who make a difference

Take a moment to think about a few of your jobs and the coworkers who made a positive difference to you. Who was shining the way?

Do not think about the jerks who made your life miserable with game playing and passive aggressive tactics. Resist the urge to give power to these negative people from your past (or even your present). Move past the bad feelings and focus on positive people—the ones

---

8   The Center for Compassion and Altruism Research and Education (CCARE) http://ccare.stanford.edu/tag/ccare/

who uplift you. It might be a kind trainer whose encouraging words taught you great skills or a human resource person who had to deliver difficult news of a layoff, but did so in a compassionate way.

Your favorite person might be a coworker who always had time to smile and wish you well, a wise boss who helped you grow, or a maintenance guy who seemed to love helping others.

Think about why you admire these positive people. Is it their humor, intelligence, or patience? Do they radiate a glow that inspired you? I think you'll realize each of these folks made an effort to relate soul to soul with the people around them, and that made all the difference. People who shine their Light at work are energized, innovative, and have more fun.

A pioneer of thought business pioneers was the late Stephen Covey, author of *7 Habits of Highly Effective People*.[9] Although he passed away in July of 2012, Stephen's teachings still inspire millions of people worldwide. Dr. Covey wrote about transition people—those who make fundamental changes to the world. Although he doesn't mention luminosity in this quote, he's referring to people who are not afraid to shine their light to better their world:

> "A transition person is one who breaks the flow of bad—the negative traditions or harmful practices that get passed from generation to generation, or from situation to situation, whether in a family, a workplace, a community, or wherever. Transition persons transcend their own needs and tap into the deepest, most noble impulses of human nature. In times of darkness, they are lights, not judges; models, not critics. In periods of discord, they are change catalysts, not victims; healers, not carriers. Today's world needs more transition persons. Trust yourself to become one of the best, and watch your influence grow."

It is within our personal power to be that "transition person," a catalyst of positive change. The fact that you're reading this book tells me you have the ability to recognize and appreciate Light when

---

9   Stephen Covey, *The 7 Habits of Highly Effective People: Powerful Lessons in Personal Change*, Rosetta Books, November 15, 2013.

you see it in others. You also have the ability to project your own Light at work, at home, and everywhere else in your world. When we bring the best of ourselves to the table, whether in the boardroom or the breakfast nook, we can create happier lives for ourselves and others. The next time you see a colleague struggle, share your experience, skills, and radiance for the greater good of the team. Illumination leads to positive integration, leaving no one stranded in the dark.

> *"Strange to say, the luminous world is the invisible world; the luminous world is that which we do not see. Our eyes of flesh see only night."*
> —Victor Hugo

Our body of light—the subtle energy system

As a holistic practitioner, I would be remiss if I didn't share information on the subtle energy system, which encompasses all living things. Including you!

When I talk about our *Energy*, I'm referring to the power within us; our Life Force and Spirit that flows through us, in us, and around us. This is the Source of our internal Light. Athletes often refer to being "in the zone," when they feel their energy system working in proper alignment with the body and mind. Business magnates the world over speak of a deep knowingness, strength, and intuition that kick in during critical negotiations. Donald Trump, famous business tycoon and a strong believer in gut instincts has said, "Without passion you don't have energy, without energy you have nothing."

The belief in this system is accepted in a great many cultures worldwide, where energy is recognized by different names, such as Prana, Ki, and Chi. Even some children's video games use these terms to display the power levels of the character playing the game.

"My power is low, I need more Chi!"

"Meditate, dude, meditate!"

This is an actual statement from my friend's son, Robbie while playing a martial arts video game. So if you haven't heard these terms, then ask a ten-year-old who can probably give you a quick lesson on the importance of Prana—especially when battling the forces of evil.

The scientific study of energy is rapidly growing, as scientists learn to detect, measure, and monitor something we can appreciate in our hearts, yet is often unseen by the naked eye.

Do a web search on "energy psychology" or "life force energy research" and you'll find hundreds of articles and studies. If you're still skeptical, which is healthy to a point, be open to learning about this. You can decide later whether or not you incorporate the wisdom I'm going to discuss. When you strive to live and work in the Light, the subtle energy system is a crucial element.

Your individual subtle energy system interacts with and processes universal energy. Whether you're with co-workers, family, and even pets, your energy fields are thrown together, giving and sending signals to each other at all times. We are all connected on a fantastic matrix of energy. Have you worked with someone so closely that you can finish each other's sentences, or come up with the same ideas at the same time? Your energy fields are sharing what exists on more subtle levels.

Energy reading lets us sense, the moment we walk into a room, that something nasty is about to "hit the fan." We feel it with our subtle energy system. Our physical bodies allow us to relate to the physical world and our energetic bodies handle the energy we encounter. Our subtle energy system has three primary sub-systems: *an energy field, energy pathways*, and *energy centers*.

The energy field, also identified as the biofield or aura, surrounds all living things and provides clues to our wellness. Plants and animals also have energy fields. Think of this field as a multi-dimensional radiant pool of energy that envelops you and extends dozens of feet beyond your body. Some people, like myself, are energy sensitive and can perceive the aura with their eyes, while others sense it through intuition or the mind's eye. When I first began to see energy, I thought I was starting to have a migraine headache and was relieved to discover I had a new, fun way of seeing. Energy abilities such as this are natural and can emerge in your life at any point. They can be developed like any other skill with determination and effort.

Energy pathways, also known as meridians or nadis, are the channels by which energies flow within our subtle energy system. These pathways are as intricate, complex, and extensive as the physical body's nervous or circulatory system. In fact, these channels form a web that connects and communicates with hundreds of energy centers within us, distributing subtle energy signals to all organs and major systems of our physical bodies.

Energy centers commonly referred to as chakras are the central points of energy activity in our bodies and subtle energy systems. The chakras are responsible for exploring, decoding, and processing the energy we come across. I like to think of these crucial centers as precious gems rooted in our energetic bodies that pulsate, spin, and glow with incredible vibrant hues. If you attend a yoga class or martial arts instruction, you'll often hear about "alignment of the chakras" or "flow of the Ki" in your body.

Energy is already a player in our lives, at work and at home, whether we discern it or not. So why not employ this knowledge for our own advantage by creating a profession and a life in energetic alignment?

Embracing the importance of Light in our lives, Mark Gerardi, a friend and fellow energy practitioner, has named his professional healing practice *Luminous and Healthy*[10]. He explains on his website,

> "Since ancient times it has been known that there is a Luminous Energy Field that surrounds the physical body. It is sometimes referred to as the light body or aura. When the human body is healthy these energy centers are clear and spin at a specific rate or vibration and the energy flows unhindered. Throughout our daily lives, stresses, be they mental, emotional, physical or spiritual, can leave their mark on our energy system as negativity in our aura."

---

10 Mark Gerardi, Luminous and Healthy, http://www.luminousandhealthy.com/

The goal of professionals like Mark is to help clients open blockages in the light body so the luminous energy may flow freely, allowing the body to return to its natural healthy state. If you haven't had the opportunity to see a professional practitioner like Mark Gerardi, treat yourself. I encourage you to experience the bliss of a direct session from a seasoned healer. It just may open your eyes to a new way of shining your Light!

In my first book, *Intuitive Parenting: Listening to the Wisdom of Your Heart*[11], I write extensively about the subtle energy system and the benefits of energy healing and energy communication for the entire family. So, if intuitive and metaphysical perspectives of energy resonate with you, please seek out the book as a resource of additional information and instruction on do-it-yourself energy techniques.

The acceptance and understanding of energy is expanding in our world. Even large corporations have begun to add onsite holistic and energy healing, such as Reiki, Tai Chi, and meditation classes to reduce workplace stress. The mind-body-spirit connection is becoming an accepted mainstream belief. It took us a few thousand years, but we've come a long way!

"I like light, color, luminosity. I like things full of color and vibrant."
—Oscar de la Renta

Light the way for good

I know some of you may fear I've fallen off the hippy-dippy deep end with my lessons on glowing hearts and light filled bodies. This is terminology I'm comfortable using freely, but I understand it isn't always familiar or easy for others.

A young woman I recently worked with while training at the insurance company asked me what I meant by "heart-centered" after I spoke about the charity I founded. One of the missions of *The HeartGlow Center* is to educate and inspire others to live their

---

11 Debra Snyder, *Intuitive Parenting: Listening to the Wisdom of Your Heart*, Atria Books/Beyond Words (May 11, 2010).

best lives—with their hearts set to glow, so they may achieve optimal happiness and health despite challenging circumstances, such as a disability or loss of a loved one. We foster living a heart-centered life, where Love is the most important path to inspired wellness.

Well, you would have thought I had two heads after I gave a similar explanation to the people in our training class. "Oh, that's interesting," she said softly and turned back to her computer screen. I laughed at myself, realizing I must have seemed like an alien from outer space. Don't these people watch *Oprah*?

Although mainstream media and talk shows seem to do more and more programming on alternative health and spiritual topics, it hasn't quite penetrated the iron walls of big business and politics. Holistic practitioners are often lumped in the "artsy" category as opposed to the "science" category. I could care less about how they try to box me in, as these limited paradigms mean little to me these days. If people think LOVE is "weird," then I am proud to be weird. As my friend Suzanne and I joke, "we're proudly waving our freak flag!"

Seriously, why would we want to live in a limiting society that dictates the manner in which we can love and do good deeds in this world? It shouldn't be wrong to be a loving person, to care about others, and support open expression and healing. What *does* frighten me is a world dictated by currency and power, with political and healthcare systems so out of whack that big business and pharmaceutical companies have more influence on our healthcare than we do.

We must wake up, take off the dark shroud being placed over us, and shine our authentic Lights in the face of darkness. We make up our world. We are points of Light. Regardless of where we are and what we're doing, we have the freedom to shine freely.

As with the other components of CALM, we can do certain things to reach our goal of luminosity, while other behaviors are better left in the past. In the next section I'll talk about simple actions in the present moment that either extinguish or ignite our spark. These mini-lessons and activities give you an opportunity to move forward in your own personal evolution.

We all have great intentions for our life, but often, after putting down a self-help book or attending a motivational event, we slip back into old, comfortable habits. If you'd like to know how to incorporate changes into your daily life, start right here with these illuminating, and sometimes provocative, suggestions.

Ignite Luminosity

Don't Surrender Your Power: We've established that we all have a powerful light within us. Each of us has a unique radiance and we each determine how and when we will shine. Why dim your glow to yield to the will of another? Unchecked egos and people living in fear try to control and dim the brilliance of others. Don't stand for it! Our combined Light makes the world a brighter place, and everyone deserves the right to shine.

Don't Compromise Your Principles: When we act in a manner opposing our personal values and beliefs, we create blockages to our luminosity. Imagine throwing a heavy blanket on a beautiful glowing orb. You won't be able to see its Light or feel its warmth as it tries to penetrate the dense fog of guilt, resentment, and discontent. On the job, a bad situation can get worse. Although we don't always have a choice regarding a decision the boss makes, expressing our truth is important.

Don't Engage Negativity: In nearly every workplace you'll find people who thrive on creating a negative atmosphere and drama. They love to poke the bear and start rumors. Why should we take part? We shouldn't. Rise above the fray and remain stable in your luminosity. A positive atmosphere is more productive than a negative one. Life is short; we spend roughly 100,000 hours of our lives on the job, so it's best to make that time as pleasant as possible.

Don't Play the Blame Game: We're often tempted to withdraw from responsibility for a situation by projecting blame onto another person or circumstance. When we blame others we're trying to deflect negative judgment from ourselves. In fact, by blaming, we often create more negativity and competition in our environment. Own your actions, good and bad, learning from the opportunities they bring forth. Exuding integrity fosters it in others.

Don't Avoid Goals: A sure fire way to fail in accomplishing your goals is to limit even having them. Have we become so jaded and exhausted from working hard that we no longer have ambition for the future? Let's snap out of it and set some goals! We, in America, have more opportunity than most other people in the world. Look at all you have going for you and the talents you were blessed with. Do not deprive us of your unique Light!

Don't Fear Your Own Grace: Do we really fear being nice? Yes, many people do, because they believe kindness, generosity, and altruism show weakness and not strength, especially in the workforce. We're taught to be ruthless, competitive, and unfeeling to achieve our goals. This is exactly where society goes wrong and why we need to change. In every brilliant, chaotic moment of life, we must bring forth the best of ourselves to realize true happiness.

Dare to be a Muse: When we gloriously shine our Light, we are not only a benefit to ourselves, but also an inspiration to others. Imagine an artist captivated by your radiance, composing a song or creating a painting divinely inspired by you. We are meant to *move* each other, to let our relationships ignite shifts in consciousness and behavior. Close your eyes and feel the resonance of this truth in your heart. Our Light holds everything beautiful about us. You, indeed, are exquisite.

Rediscover Your Faith: What does being a person of faith mean to you? Is it belief in yourself, or maybe a higher power? Look at where you place your trust and faith. When all else fails, this is what you can count on. Include more of that in your life. If you only trust your dog, spend more time with dogs. Be an animal trainer or volunteer at a shelter. If you value your church, go more often and take a larger role. All authentic belief leads to greater self-understanding.

Raise Your Vibration: Yes, we're speaking my energy language again. This is easy to do, because we simply need to find what uplifts us, what ignites our spirit. The answer is different for everyone, because we are all uniquely the same. (Bonus points if you get that!) Go for a run. Sing a song. Make Love. Swim. Call an old friend and laugh about your wild adventures. Raising our vibration clears away the debris that has collected in our light body. It feels sensational to lighten our load.

Explore Energy Healing: This is your opportunity to do something nice for yourself and discover ancient techniques. Schedule a session with a professional for a relaxing energy massage, meditation circle, or Reiki healing. Ask a friend for a reference or research a holistic education center near you. Go in with an open heart and mind. Even if you're skeptical, give it an honest try. I bet you'll be pleasantly surprised by the positive, nurturing experience of energy healing and will go back for more.

Embrace Silence: One of the best gifts I ever gave myself was the permission to be quiet; to not fill every moment with noise and the sound of my own voice. When we embrace silence, we hear others more and can respond consciously with sincerity. Silence also allows us to hear our inner voice of intuition, the sound our Light emanates. Allow the chaos and clutter of a noisy world to drift away by sitting in silence at least ten minutes a day.

Share your Radiance: When you grasp your light from the inside, why be afraid to show it? Look for opportunities to shine at work, at home, and in your community. No matter our age, weight, race, finances, profession—you name it—we can each give freely of ourselves to others. By being a beacon in our world and shining our own Light, we encourage others to do the same. Imagine the beauty of our world if we all had our hearts set to glow.

Ignition points

- You hear about it all the time: random acts of kindness, where people do something nice for strangers. Have you joined the fun? Today, light up someone's life with a good deed. Open a door, carry a bag, or buy a lunch. Make a donation, help clean up a public area, or volunteer at a local charity. Nothing strengthens your Light faster than doing good deeds for others.
- Take an energy inventory of your possessions. Go through your home, asking yourself "Does this item uplift me?" If it doesn't, consider letting it go. Many times clutter in our world drains us and keeps us stuck in a rut.

Chapter Four Exercise—Ignite CALM

What makes your heart glow?

Our hearts do glow and have an energy field of their own, proven and measured by scientific instruments. Our hearts hold our Light, our Love. They are intuitive and communicative. If you listen, your heart can lead you to a fantastic life. In this simple exercise, I urge you to begin listening to your heart and understanding how your body processes your genuine emotions energetically. This level of communication is priceless, as it can lead you closer and closer to your true path. In fact, it will allow you to determine if your profession is worth holding onto or releasing.

Find a quiet place in your home where you can be alone for ten minutes or so. I strive to have our exercises be flexible; you can do smaller versions to start, and then expand your exploration over time as you become more comfortable and truly enjoy doing them. Sit upright in a comfortable chair with your feet on the ground. Take a deep breath and close your eyes. Simply *be* for a moment or two as you settle in and tune out distractions of the external environment. We will be focusing inward.

Take another deep, cleansing breath through your nose and then exhale out your mouth. Repeat this a few times. With your eyes still closed, think about someone you dearly love. Picture every detail of this person's face, his or her whole being. Think positive, loving thoughts of this person, allowing yourself to smile at memories of your cherished time together. Now, focus on the feeling in your chest. How does your heart feel? How does your body feel? Do you have butterflies in your stomach or tingling in your fingers? What else do you feel?

Repeat this visualization, but now replace the image of your loved one with something you fear. It could be spiders or snakes or a negative memory from childhood. Now again, focus on the feeling in your chest. How does your heart feel? What other sensations do you have in your body?

Again think of a loving image, a person or thing that makes you happy. Make note of any changes you perceive within yourself. Open your eyes and come back to the present moment. Write down any reflections you have from this exercise. Congratulate yourself for opening a dialogue with your heart center. Actually, this communication is constant, but we aren't always aware of it. Now you are. This is where we get the phrases "gut instinct" and "heartfelt."

Now that you can recognize the subtle sensations of your energy body, take a moment to tap into your heart center in regard to your profession and activities of daily living. In your mind's eye, picture yourself doing your work. This can be what pays you a check or the many tasks you do at home and for others. As you see the scenes before you, how does your body feel? Do you have a tight feeling anywhere in your body? How does your jaw feel? Is your stomach swirling or calm? Out of the duties you're exploring do some make you feel better or worse? Maybe your heart is telling you driving a truck is preferred over doing paperwork. What makes you feel uplifted or deflated?

Challenge yourself with new situations and scenarios to get to the heart of the matter, always following the energy that feels positive to you, while making note of what is less desirable. I suggest you repeat this exercise often and test yourself with different topics and questions, such as issues with your family or what adventures you should take. You can even do this as a group of people and discuss your results afterward. Learning to tap into your powerful Light body can positively shift your experiences and lead to a rich life of luminosity.

Chapter Five
Mindfulness

"Mindfulness is about love and loving life. When you cultivate this love, it gives you clarity and compassion for life, and your actions happen in accordance with that."
—Jon Kabat-Zinn

THE FOURTH AND FINAL component in our CALM approach is mindfulness, the in-the-moment awareness of your feelings, sensations, thoughts, and surroundings. When being mindful, we are not judging something as right or wrong; rather we accept things as they come without projecting our history or our future into the equation. We live in and for that moment. We live for today.

Let's face it, most of us habitually dwell in thoughts of yesterday, or we're always caught up in dreams and goals for tomorrow. We lose the importance and excitement of the present moment. The miracles are in the moment, my friends, coming one at a time. By being consciously aware of the present, we empower ourselves with the highest level of understanding and the ability to create a life of peace and wellness.

Although mindfulness originates from time-honored Buddhist teachings, these valuable practices are available to everyone, regardless of our spiritual beliefs or religious activities. Techniques of mindfulness are used in therapy-based programs to promote stress reduction, treat behavioral issues such as anxiety and depression, and tackle substance abuse. The clarity you achieve through mindfulness can enhance an already robust and dedicated way of being. With its detailed focus on mental development, mindfulness can be a crucial tool for managing occupational challenges, as well as facing struggles in all areas of life: body, mind, and spirit.

The father of modern mindfulness would have to be Jon Kabat-Zinn.[12] He teaches mindfulness and Mindfulness-Based Stress Reduction (MBSR) in a variety of settings around the world and is the author of numerous scientific papers on the applications of mindfulness in health care and medicine. He has educated our world about the benefits of mindfulness by authoring numerous books, translated into over thirty languages and has provided mindfulness training to people in diverse professions including: CEOs, clergy, judges, and professional athletes.

Research on mindfulness shows a full range of benefits, from boosting our immune system to improving the way we parent our children. Talk about win-win! Studies have primarily centered on the mind-body interactions for healing, clinical applications of mindfulness training, and its effects on the brain, the immune system, and on stress and emotional expression. Mindfulness has now moved into mainstream institutions such as medicine, psychology, health care, and schools, as well as exploring stress in corporate environments and work situations.

Research on mindfulness at work showed a distinct connection between workplace mindfulness and performance success on the job. The study was a major step forward as it looked at effects on average workers and not only corporate leaders.[13] Mindfulness is not only for

---

12 Kabat-Zinn is the founding Executive Director of the Center for Mindfulness in Medicine, Health Care, and Society at the University of Massachusetts Medical School as well as the Stress Reduction Clinic at the University of Massachusetts Medical School.
13 Erik Dane and Bradley J Brummel, "Examining workplace mindfulness and its relations to job performance and turnover intention," *Human Relations* 2014 67: 105 originally published online 3 June 2013

those high on the chain of command. All parties in the workforce, regardless of hierarchy, can utilize mindfulness to foster a productive and profitable environment.

Why is mindfulness hard?

So let's spell this out. By being mindful AND embracing ourselves authentically, we can achieve greater happiness in the workplace. We are more fulfilled, productive, and profitable.

In truth, it is a simple concept.

When we are mindful, positive, active, and properly utilized, the benefits to the employee and employer are magnified.

So why does this seem so hard sometimes?

It's hard because we make it that way. Simply look at the reverse of what I said above:

When we are negative, disengaged, overworked, or underutilized, there are few benefits to the employee and employer, causing a reduction in productivity and profits.

Toxic emotions disrupt the workplace. We all realize when things start to go downhill, they pick up steam fast. Let's break away from the old worn habits of fostering negative environments and, together, create situations we can all be proud of. Doing great work is good for the soul. Any job can be our dream job when you're fully present in every moment. I'll explain more about that during this chapter.

I realize these concepts put pressure on businesses to make solid changes—and changes by the employees too. Guess what? Change is vastly needed. We have already learned it will benefit everyone involved, so it's time to ignite our innovation and ingenuity to make a positive, mindful difference in the workplace.

When looking at the potential benefits of mindfulness on the job, we can clearly see the opportunities available for directors and employees in how they handle interactions. In one of my rough work moments, I confided in my supervisor that I was working longer hours than I anticipated, and therefore I needed to be careful and manage my time better. I thought I was being proactive by making an honest statement and looking for her suggestions on better managing my workflow. Her reply?

"You're going to make me look bad!"

Not exactly the support and encouragement I was looking for while I was just out of the training room and already feeling overwhelmed. Her own fear of inadequacy and future repercussions from her superiors made this simple moment so much worse than it had to be. That conversation marked the beginning of the end for me, because after this, neither of us had faith and respect for the other. Had I been more mindful in that moment, I would have addressed her "look bad" comment right then, or tried not to take it personally. If she had been more mindful, she wouldn't have said it in the first place. Perhaps she could have addressed my concerns in a more detached, mutually respectful manner. Instead, we both stewed on it overnight, causing the toxicity to grow and lead to my formal, abrupt departure the very next day. In a way, her comment became a self-fulfilling prophecy.

> *"We need to awaken ourselves. We need to practice mindfulness if we want to have a future, if we want to save ourselves and the planet."*
> —Thich Nhat Hanh

Companies doing the right thing

Many successful companies are leading the way in designing collaborative and conscious workplaces. For example, Google and General Mills have incorporated the concept of mindfulness to create foster a more positive and profitable workplace. Through courses on meditation, self-development, and conscious team building, these groups are reaping the rewards of happier employees and increased productivity. Other *mindful* firms include:

- Apple
- McKinsey & Company
- Deutsche Bank
- Proctor and Gamble
- Astra Zeneca
- Green Mountain Coffee Roasters
- Target

An article in *Financial Times* described the growth of mindfulness and discussed General Mills' commitment to making it part of their culture. Among other findings, "...the early results are striking... And among senior executives who took the course, 80 percent reported a positive change in their ability to make better decisions, while 89 percent said they became better listeners."[14]

There are no reliable statistics on how many companies promote mindfulness in the workplace, but 25 percent of large employers in the United States have launched stress reduction programs. Although this trend is a positive sign, we cannot rely solely upon our employers to manifest mindfulness. This is something only we can create from within. We must challenge ourselves to take the necessary steps and create an atmosphere in which we can truly thrive.

Years ago I worked with Tom, a pleasant, talented man who was near the top of his profession in experience and skills. He was the person to investigate the most challenging disability claims and his decades in the field made him a tremendous resource. Unfortunately, somewhere along the way Tom became disgruntled and totally burned out on his job from lack of balance in his life. Spending hours each day complaining about his workload, he wandered from cubicle to cubicle looking for support and someone to bitch and kibitz with about the company. Although some of his concerns were valid, he could not see that by breeding discontent and wasting time wandering around, he was making the situation worse for himself

---

14 David Gelles "The Mind Business," Financial Times, August 24, 2012 http://dld.bz/dxZEZ

as calls and emails backed up. Other members of the team would head in the opposite direction when they heard him coming—and this contributed even more to his feelings of isolation and injustice.

Tom, like many others in a similar situation, was misdirecting his energy and surrendering his own power. If he'd taken action on his concerns by scheduling a meeting with his supervisors, perhaps he could've brokered a solution to his problems, such as a reduction in his workload, a shift to a new position, or even an extended vacation to rejuvenate his spirit. By remaining the victim of circumstance, Tom garnered the attention he craved; unfortunately it was negative attention. His years of solid service were undermined when he became a troublesome malcontent.

A commitment to mindfulness

Once we make a commitment to become more mindful, to take each moment as it comes with keen awareness and responsibility, then all aspects of our lives start coming together. When we acutely observe, allowing the energy of each moment to be expressed fully, we understand more than the average person. Yes, we become more intuitive and downright sharp.

The instant urge of our ego to strike back in defense of our position is silenced, because we feel confident and secure in ourselves and will select the proper time to speak. You can test this right now by observing a conversation or a meeting at work. While watching from the sidelines it's easy to see how everyone could interact in a more constructive manner. Did you see how no one could hear what the other person was saying because they talked over each other? And look at that body language!

When we are being mindful in a conversation, we are the participant AND the observer at the same time. A fun way to look at this is through the eyes of a professional poker player. Sharply aware of the surroundings, our player takes all things into consideration during every second of the game: the hand that was dealt, bets on the table, every look and sound coming from the other players, as well as how everything interacts and changes through each round and the entire game. We know the player can't jump for joy at first sight of a great hand or grimace at a poor one—that would tip off the other players. Emotions are felt, yet kept in check for the proper moment of expression, usually a huge smile while capturing the pot at the end. Poker can be a metaphor for the unlimited possibilities in life. We have infinite scenarios, a full cast of characters to interact with, and spectacular potential taking shape moment-to-moment, all vastly improved by our awareness. Heightened awareness of your world can make the difference between a so-so life and a great one. Why settle for so-so?

Sometimes it's easier to learn about mindfulness when you see what mindfulness is not. Tragedy strikes in our world every day from actions taken when we are unaware, preoccupied, and forgetful. Our society has even developed new laws to address the crisis of "distracted drivers" who cause accidents or injury due to inattentiveness while behind the wheel. A driver who's sending a text message, applying make-up, or eating a snack has lost sight of his primary purpose—safely operating a large and dangerous machine.

In our busy lives, our attention can be diverted from "real life" by hundreds of things, including gaming, sports, drinking, sex, television, and social networking. Yes, Facebook, I mean you! All of these activities can be wonderful in the proper time and place. However, allowing ourselves to be consumed by any one thing creates a danger to the other things in life we care about. We must achieve balance.

How many times have you heard a friend complain about her husband who works all the time? Or of an ex-husband who's too busy to spend time with the kids? Are you too busy to call your family or spend quality time with them? Life can easily get out of whack and turn into a bizarre circle if we aren't careful. Often we work too much, which is so exhausting that we need to zone out in front of the TV or have a drink at the end of a long, busy day, which then leaves us too tired to read to the kids before bed. Our children cope with their loneliness by playing video games. All this makes it difficult to get out of the house as a family on the weekends, creating more stress. And on and on it goes. This might not be your exact scenario, but I bet you recognize the life pattern of a friend or neighbor. No one wants this fruitless situation, but how do we stop?

Mindfulness is a celebration of life, when you savior every succulent moment. It is not a chore. It is a blessing and a freedom. Think back to the first time you set eyes on someone you were attracted to and remember the tingle you felt. The energy of that moment is etched in your heart and mind forever, because you recognized the magic. Realize how many magical moments you're allowing to slip away, unnoticed.

Take a minute right now to reflect on a departed loved one you desperately miss; a parent, grandparent, colleague, or dear friend. How many times since their passing have you wished for one more moment to hold a hand, hear a voice, or simply feel that person's energy beside you? The gift of everything we hold dear is tenderly held in each precious moment. When we fully awaken to the beauty and significance of our lives, nothing is ever the same. We fall in love with creation again and again.

By bringing our attention to the present moment, we live and love fully. We respect and understand our true nature and values. We have fewer regrets, because we live with purpose and on purpose. Our tears and our laughter are authentically felt and expressed. All the things we cherish at home and at work blend together harmoniously. When we're on the job, we focus on what we are doing, secure in our minds that our efforts help create a prosperous, meaningful life for our families. When we're at home, we enjoy the people we adore and take pleasure in things we like to do, leaving the stress of the office or assembly line behind.

It makes no sense to hold a job that holds you hostage. If your job is costing you your life, then leave it. Your treasure is not hidden in a high salary, a posh corner office, or even in a luxury car. You'll discover riches are secured in the smile of your child, the caresses of love, and the creative expression of your own spirit.

As with the other components of CALM, there are things you can do to support mindfulness in your life. There are also poor habits that will keep you locked into an outdated paradigm, asleep at the wheel of life. Each of us gets to decide how we live our lives—whether we choose to be active and aware or remain in a haze, simply going through the motions in hopes something will improve without our involvement.

Here are activities that can extinguish or ignite the light of mindfulness in your world. Make a commitment to see how they resonate in your life.

Ignite Mindfulness

Don't hold your breath: By holding our breath, we attempt to make time stand still. We resist the truth of the present moment, rejecting the reality of what we must face. In fact, it's a good idea to count your breaths as you allow your body and mind to connect in the present moment. Whatever that moment brings. Breathe into each second fully, allowing the rhythm of your breath to bring you comfort in your present state.

Don't check out of life: This is an easy trap to fall into. Many of us withdraw out of self-protection. We hide from responsibilities at work and home by creating an alternate safe reality, usually some form of escape, such as reading, gaming, or watching TV. None of these pastimes are problems until they keep you from experiencing fully what the world has to offer. If you find many of your moments are exactly the same, then its time to change things up.

Don't judge yourself or others: When we embrace mindfulness, we are not judge and jury of what's occurring in the moment. We strive to be present with what is and allow emotions to rise and fall naturally without the added projection of being "good" or "bad." By simply existing in conscious awareness, we allow the full energy of a situation to unfold, letting our presence enrich the experience instead of limiting it.

Don't be a cling-on: Becoming attached is so easy. Whether to people, places, things, roles, or ideas, attachment stems from fear. Allow the flow of life's circumstances to surround you without hanging on to any one thing. You have the ability to adapt to every situation and the resilience to weather uncertainty. If you find yourself without a job or your responsibilities at work are shifting, recognize with confidence that you can handle it.

Don't live in the past: We miss the beauty of the present moment when we're blinded by the ghosts in our past. Our history can color how we look at things and also get in the way of enjoying new experiences. Be where you are in the now. Every encounter in life makes us who we are, so rely on the "who" you have become now, not who you were yesterday. Honor the past, yet live in the now.

Don't think only of the future: We see it all the time: Honest, hard-working people who live years ahead of where they are in the present moment. Often with admirable goals, they squirrel and fight, say no to adventures to save money, and keep on a focused trail. The problem is, by living only for tomorrow, you deny yourself the gift of today. Many of us never make it to retirement. Don't be the one to look up from your desk one day and discover the children have already grown up and your spouse left on that adventure without you.

Go with the flow: Life becomes an exciting journey when we learn to go with the flow, rising and falling in every moment like a surfer navigating beautiful waves. This type of life isn't just for Bohemians; it can be for you too. Accept with a spirit of adventure the diverse experiences that come your way. Opportunities will find you when you open your arms to welcome them.

Know your body: The first step to a life of mindfulness can begin in your own skin. Practice being in the moment by tapping into your body and sensing how you feel, physically and emotionally. Sit in a comfortable chair or relax on your bed and take an awareness tour of your body. What do your ears hear? What do your eyes see and how well do they see it? Talk to your muscles and your bones. Discover the beautiful complexity of your form.

Open your eyes: We will never run out of things to see in this beautiful world. But do we truly look? Sadly, most of us do not. We are typically on autopilot and we go through our days without fully appreciating the exquisite beauty and gritty reality that is our world. Sit by an open window and gaze upon the view. Take in each color, every blade of grass, and all the tiny details of what you see. I bet you will learn a few things.

The miracles in the moment: When making the commitment to be mindful, we begin by meeting each moment as it comes in active awareness. We must be present and engaged, not falling asleep from boredom. To get yourself in good practice, imagine how you would describe the moment to someone else with every detail intact. Allow your senses to pick up all information, taking everything in, to understand the depth of the situation and the miracle of the moment.

Celebrate connections: When we are mindful, we live in celebration of our connectedness to all other things. We understand we are part of nature, part of society, part of a family and yes, even part of a company. Seeing how all things are related and mutually dependent allows us deep reflection and gratitude for our life and our place in the cycle. We have greater empathy and understanding for the people we encounter, for we are just like them, all magnificent interconnected pieces of the puzzle.

Embrace what is: As the adage says, "it is what it is" and that is all it can ever be. By accepting what is without attachment or projection, we are free from our own limitations and can reduce our suffering. Exploding in a rage or hysterical tears will not un-ring the bell ... or get our jobs back. Companies downsize, people get fired, and partners sometimes leave us. Our desired outcome for a situation is not always its reality. You have done it before and will do it again; you have the strength to face what is difficult.

Ignition points

- Take time to meditate and connect with the higher parts of you. Simply sitting for a few moments at the beginning and end of each day can soothe a tattered spirit.
- Forgive yourself. Right now in this very moment release the burden of guilt you have been carrying in your heart for past missteps, hurts, and wrongs. From this moment on, you will be more mindful in your actions and decisions.

Chapter Five Exercise – Ignite CALM

Interviewing the moment

The next exercise is a fun one, especially if you're interested in creative writing and stepping outside the box a bit. I would like you to select a joyful or special moment from your life. It could be when a child was born, when you were married, or perhaps the time you went whitewater rafting. The moment you choose is entirely up to you, but select something that makes you happy, because I want to activate positive, upbeat aspects at this point in time.

When you've identified a moment you wish to explore, I want you to reflect on it, and then write about it in immense detail. In this scenario, you are the interviewer and the one being interviewed, so I ask you to wear both hats at the same time.

You have selected your happy moment. Now, in reflection and analysis like a reporter doing a story, I want you to dig deep and get all the details, the inside scoop. When I took a journalism class in college many moons ago, they encouraged us to focus on the following:

Who,

What,

When,

Where,

Why, and

How.

You can see why reporters stick to some version of this formula, because they have a tremendous amount of information to convey in limited space and time. For our situation, we will use their tools to get the details out of a moment in time.

Using those six basic questions, begin to take notes about your positive moment, gradually fleshing out the details. For example, if you're considering a rafting trip: Who was there? What was going on? When did this happen? How did it make you feel? You can see how each simple question opens up the door for other questions and greater detail. If you knew Joe was wearing a yellow shirt, you can think back to recall the exact shade or texture ... did it have a logo or a stripe? Could you smell his cologne on the shirt collar? You get the point. Allow your amazing mind to bring forth the details.

Gather the facts and then write a brief story as if it would appear in a newspaper or a blog. You are focusing in on a moment in time: a kiss, a joke, or the bite of a delicious meal. You can make the story as long or as short as you wish. This is meant to be a positive and fun exploration and not a chore. Allow yourself to get into it. If you prefer audio or video, feel free to record your story as an on-air reporter.

Reflecting back to this moment helps us see the poignant potential in every other moment we have. At all times our minds are taking in a huge variety of information—so much stimulation that we begin to tune out and become disconnected, mindlessly going through life. Please understand we can embrace each moment in blissful awareness. Let's be in our lives *now*, fully present, expansive and open to the adventure in every moment.

Chapter Six
Simplicity

"Remembering that you are going to die is the best way I know to avoid the trap of thinking you have something to lose. You are already naked. There is no reason not to follow your heart."
—Steve Jobs

I HAVE DEVELOPED a sense of fearlessness in living my life. Maybe it comes from being the mother of a profoundly disabled child who wasn't expected to live long, but did. Or perhaps it's from witnessing friends die too young of cancer or suicide. I want to drink everything in before I pass on from this world.

We've all lost people we wish were still here with us, enjoying life. Part of me feels I would be disrespectful to my departed loved ones if I failed to appreciate the gift of life with great exuberance. In honor and celebration of their lives, I enjoy a lobster roll for my Gamma or the beauty of a boat sailing toward the sunset for my stepfather, Frank. I run barefoot in fields of flowers, something my daughter will never get to experience in her lifetime. There is much to celebrate about being alive.

If we spend our time complaining about life without taking responsibility for our actions and emotions, we are choosing a disempowered, victimized existence. We are not embracing positive actions to change our circumstances or perspective. I developed the CALM method to empower people to live life fully and allow bliss to work in all aspects of their lives, whether at home or in their professions. Seeing so many talented people suffer on the job and for their jobs made me realize how many of us have lost sight of the importance of Self in day-to-day living. We've grown accustomed to last place on the list of daily priorities—after the kids, the boss, the tedious errands, and our financial obligations. We don't recognize who we are anymore because the roles we play crowd in around us, blocking our Light.

Have you ever noticed how difficult it is to decide where to go out for dinner when we have the sole responsibility for making that decision? It should be a fun choice, yet being disconnected from our Self, and also our taste buds, leaves us whining and complaining about having the burden to choose. Children would shout "Pizza! Spaghetti!" or whatever else they might be craving. What has happened to our childlike excitement for living? Fortunately, it's in there ... somewhere. We need only give ourselves the time, space, and attention to allow the fire of our souls to ignite into playful expression again. Remember, when we are at our best, in full radiance, we are of greater service to others at work, home, and in all endeavors we pursue.

Earlier chapters specifically explored the individual components of CALM: Creativity, Authenticity, Luminosity, and Mindfulness. Now we'll delve into how you can apply this method in the everyday work situations and scenarios of your life. You'll also learn the best ways to support CALM once you make the commitment to incorporate it into many aspects of daily living, including how you live, your ability to make money, and your talents as a leader and innovator.

In the first chapter exercise I presented the CALM technique, questions you should go to when facing a decision or challenge. This technique encourages you to ignite CALM by getting into a clear state when looking at the situations of your life. Now that you have a greater understanding of the individual components and how they work in your life, you're ready to more fully discover the magic of this approach. This is your go-to technique whenever you feel burdened and need to find a solution. There are no right and wrong answers. The important point is that you're asking these questions to welcome YOUR truth.

Ignite CALM:	To ignite CALM, ask yourself four simple questions and be absolutely honest in your answers.
Creativity:	Have I looked at this situation creatively?
Authenticity:	Am I being true to my personal values and goals?
Luminosity:	Am I bringing the best of me to this issue?
Mindfulness:	How does this situation affect my life and others?

Can you see how your greater understanding of the individual components of CALM will enrich the answers to these questions? You've learned the depth of being creative and authentic. You appreciate what luminosity and mindfulness truly are. If you get stuck at any point, go back to the earlier chapter for a fresh perspective and ignition point suggestions.

I am presenting this expansive life philosophy in a friendly, but not always easy, manner. Yes, things that push our buttons aren't always easy. Perhaps you've grown accustomed to being a worker bee, focused only on tasks and ignoring the expression of your spirit. Taste the honey of life by doing it all at the same time. We can be happy worker bees, creatively buzzing about, each of us making the world a better place.

> *"If you think dealing with issues like worthiness and authenticity and vulnerability are not worthwhile because there are more pressing issues, like the bottom line or attendance or standardized test scores, you are sadly, sadly mistaken. It underpins everything."*
> —Brene Brown

The freedom of simplicity

Somewhere along the way we have lost ourselves and become disconnected from our purpose. We have gone astray from what truly matters. Instead, we fill our lives with clutter in hopes it will fulfill us on some level. Yearning for inner peace, we struggle and strive to create a world of happiness dependent on the "things" we acquire; things we're conditioned to believe hold value in society. Whether it's the latest gadget or gizmo, a huge house in the hills, or an advanced beauty cream; our lives become consumed with the act of consumption. We work at stressful jobs we don't like, to feed our spending habits, in desperate hopes it will bring happiness to ourselves and those we love. The retail giants label us perfectly as "consumers," people who acquire things to be used for their own purposes. Yuck. What a horrible way to be described—and not a pleasant way to live.

We cannot expect our life's thirst to be quenched by something that is dry, empty, and devoid of energy. *Things* are just things. It is time to realize our personal value is not determined by driving a Lexus or having the latest iPhone. A thing does not create the emotional state we desire. We want to feel loved, accepted, secure, and comforted, but we mistakenly attempt to satisfy those needs with objects instead of self-actualization. A society that values money over self-worth has habituated us to this behavior. Fearing we ARE only what we possess, we constantly strive to possess more.

An engagement ring on its own is only an object, metal and stone. What we crave is the loving energy this ring represents. Yet somehow we confuse the item for the feeling itself. If the ring cost two months' salary, then it must represent more love. The marketing experts win as they tap into our anxiety:

"She won't know I love her if the ring isn't big enough."

Or, "He must not value me because this ring is cheap."

We allow ourselves to be manipulated by the greed of others. Only we can stop this by determining for ourselves what it is we truly value. If we can assert our intention onto any item or action, why must it only be linked to luxury or vast quantities? Can any pebble on the shore or an act of service convey our energy? Yes, it can. If we identify our desires, we can fulfill our needs and express ourselves without the attachment to something outside the self.

Recently my friend received a bicycle as an engagement gift from her fiancé, instead of a diamond ring. They were both turned off by the politics and scandal surrounding the diamond industry. The bike represents their shared values and expresses their sincere intention to spend time doing something they both enjoy. The value coming from the emotion behind this gift was a sweet gesture of their feelings. Their love perfectly characterized by a purple Schwinn.

Although I understand the buying and selling of products and services keeps money flowing in our world, I think we can strike a better balance through conscious consumerism. Invest in what truly matters to you, leaving behind the burdensome extras projected upon us as a gateway to happiness. No need to "keep up with the Joneses," the Kardashians, or anyone else on the block. When we are mindful of our own value and our principles, we're less swayed by the concept of ownership. We are more in tune with who people are and what they do. We can discover the freedom in simplicity as we celebrate and thrive in our happy homes.

The beauty of simplicity

Stacey, a friend for over a dozen years, has always chosen to live in a small, inexpensive apartment in the working class area of town. Although with her education and background she could afford a more lavish lifestyle, she made a decision to keep her living expenses modest to allow for flexibility in other areas of her life. With her costs vastly reduced without a mortgage and zero revolving credit debt, Stacey only has to work part-time, leaving her considerable opportunities for travel, leisure, and adventures. She takes classes, goes on walks, and has the time for lunches with friends. Sounds good doesn't it? Stacey knows the freedom to simply *be* is more important to her than the high cost of an extravagant lifestyle.

Having everything she needs, Stacey's creativity and commitment to living her life simply, suit her perfectly.

Research by Brown and Kasser[15] looked at whether ecological and psychological well-being are compatible in our society. Their studies examined the roles of values, mindfulness, and lifestyle in both adolescents and adults exploring "subjective well-being and ecologically responsible behavior." The specific study on adults showed that voluntary lifestyle of simplicity was in line with higher ecologically responsible behavior. These researchers are hopeful about their findings: They conclude that by supporting our lifestyles with intrinsic values and mindfulness, we can cultivate lives that are mutually beneficial for both personal and planetary well-being.

Individual happiness and the wellness of our world may, in fact, complement one another, instead of conflict. Allowing our lives to become simpler may lead to greater joy and also a healthier world.

Simplicity means more than reducing our material possessions. We can look at many aspects of our behavior to see where we allowed ourselves to get so darned complicated.

Is it in our relationships?

The food we eat?

The activities we choose to take part in?

Is our work too much work?

I am always surprised to see the frantic running around many families do as they manage the complex lives they've created for themselves. Everyone is trying to go in numerous directions at the same time to meet overcrowded schedules. Something has to give, and it's usually their quality of life.

Simpler food

My client Pam was at wits' end because she was cooking several different versions of dinner each night to appease her children's finicky palates. Their varied requests were not due to a medical

---

15 Kirk Warren Brown and Tim Kasser, "Are Psychological and Ecological Well-Being Compatible? The Role of Values, Mindfulness, and Lifestyle," Social Indicators Research 74: 349–368, 2005

condition or allergies. She was trying to keep the peace—and becoming exhausted and broke in the process, as they often ended up doing a take-out run to several drive-thru restaurants or excessive trips to the grocery store. I think Pam deserves "Mom of the Year" for her loving efforts, yet she needs to examine how she's enabling her children into habits that may not best support their lives, especially as they get older and need to be responsible for themselves.

Food nurtures and sustains our bodies, but the choices we make on what to eat shouldn't be based on the rise and fall of emotions. Although we all know food can be fabulous and fun, keeping it simple and nutritious is best for daily living. We have plenty of celebrations on our calendars to explore fancy food. When I was growing up, if you didn't like what the family was eating, then you ate a sandwich or maybe a bowl of cereal with fruit. Believe me, I passed on the nights my mom served liver and onions or tuna noodle casserole. I did, however, develop a taste for things I didn't think I'd like, and I still have fond memories of the home cooked dishes she made with love and care. The fuel for our bodies need not be complicated. With food shortages everywhere, let us honor what we have and foster a better relationship with what nourishes us.

Living a life with less complication allows us a freedom of expression few people now experience. Years ago life was lived at a slower pace. Look at office work for example. When I was growing up in the 1970s and 80s, the technology we are currently immersed in was just starting to make an appearance. The average office worker serviced clients, did paperwork, opened the daily mail, used a typewriter, maybe had access to a basic computer, and answered the phone, usually one call at a time. If you were in a larger company, you may have multiple lines coming in but they were usually reserved for specific people. The phone lines would give a busy signal to inform the caller they needed to call back.

Today, in addition to basic activities, we have vast amounts of incoming and outgoing email correspondence to manage, multiple mail and package deliveries, social media, and unlimited phone communication on multiple phones. If we're already on the phone, the person calling gets our voicemail to leave a detailed message. While we're retrieving that message, another call comes in.

The productivity expected from employees is downright ridiculous and leaves little room to catch a breath. In less than forty short years, technology has taken over our lives and is now crowding in on our souls.

Relationships

Many people try to put all their eggs in one basket when it comes to relationships. Most often, we project the role of spouse to include best friend, lover, soul mate, mentor, confidant, sounding board, and provider all rolled up in one person. Geez ... talk about pressure! As we mature and develop strong relationships with friends, family, and colleagues, we begin to see our needs are met in beautiful creative ways that include a variety of relationships. This often benefits our marriages. My husband and I wouldn't have lasted over 26 years together if each of us tried to make each other the only answer in life. We hold the answers for our own lives. We each have different interests, explorations, and friends. We're independent, yet we choose to do many things together.

The same is true of professions. Most of us mistakenly think our jobs have to be the only thing that stimulates us and the only avenue for financial support. This fosters co-dependency and unrealistic expectations from both employers and employees. Frustration sets in as we begin resenting our jobs for overburdening or under compensating us. This attitude quickly begins to take a toll on our private lives and our souls.

If we see our careers as a single component of our lives—a way to assist us with our needs and also an opportunity to be of service to others—we will be happier employees, doing better work. We choose how many hours we work and how much space we allow a job to occupy in our heads and our hearts. Smart, happy workers in all fields have learned the secret is leaving it behind at the end of the shift, whether you're a doctor, teacher, sanitation worker, police officer, or bartender. Your job is not your life and if alterations are needed in how you work, they must begin with you.

Although we may not be able to change what's expected of us in our careers overnight, we can make changes in our lives that put things in better balance and simplify our experiences. Establishing a strong set of personal boundaries is a great place to start. Recognize what you are and are NOT willing to do at work, at home, and in your relationships. Start by setting a time at which you disconnect completely from certain responsibilities by leaving the location, unplugging your phone, and learning to say no as needed. You don't have to grab for your phone in the middle of the night each time you hear a new message chime. Hang out the "gone fishing" sign and go fishing, or golfing, or to a museum. Determine how much of your day will be all yours and stick to it. Use the CALM questions to explore how you can simplify your life in the here and now. Here are suggestions for exploring simplicity in your life:

Ignite Simplicity

Don't make it complicated: We all find ourselves making a simple act or situation more complicated than it needs to be. How many times have you had an argument with a loved one that could be resolved with a simple apology and acknowledgement of a mistake? Do apologize and leave the drama for TV. Be who you are, speak your truth, and appreciate those you share life with. The simple fact is: love isn't complicated, and if it is, maybe it isn't love after all.

Don't over think: Do you realize not everything you think should be believed? Our minds can get carried away with worries, fear, and frustration, often creating stories that belong in the fiction section, not in the present moment. When you feel a negative mental spin coming on, stop it in its tracks with an absolute fact of a positive accomplishment. By reminding yourself of the day you landed the big client or got that homerun, you will stifle the worry about what may or may not happen in tomorrow's meeting. You got this!

Don't under act: Inactivity can hurt you greatly by complicating your life. Always playing catch up from being in passive mode puts you at risk in your profession and daily responsibilities. We miss deadlines for projects, bills go unpaid, and opportunities pass us by because we aren't ready and willing to accept future prospects. At the mercy of active decision makers, we can find ourselves overwhelmed and stuck in a state of complex reactivity.

Don't point the finger: It's always easier to shift responsibility onto someone or something else. Especially in our professions, we give fault to the boss, the rude customer, an unprepared co-worker, and even the local economy. Make it simple for yourself—take on the responsibility for doing your job, the good and the bad. The personal rewards you gain from seeing a project through are like nothing else.

Don't over schedule: One the greatest challenges we all face is trying to do too much at the same time. Hey, we're talented and can do a great many things. But to be done properly, each task should have its shining moment and proper attention. Get yourself organized by dividing your tasks, meetings, and responsibilities over a longer period of time. Work never really ends, there's always something to do, so slow down and do it well.

Don't promise the moon: We've all done it: Set ourselves up for total failure at the office and at home by over promising. We like to make people happy, which is a good thing, but if it isn't our truth or within our power to deliver, then our promises only create disappointment and breed mistrust. You lose credibility when you take on burdens you aren't able to carry. People like it when you're real with them and they will value you for who you are.

Know what matters: This is one of the most important things I will ever say to you ... *you must determine what matters to you in life and then make your decisions in support of those values.* If family is the most important thing to you, then do what sustains your family. If it's your career as a trapeze artist, then join the circus. Having your priorities set allows you tremendous freedom and simplicity in your life. Your decisions come easier, because all complications become minor distractions incapable of rocking your foundation.

Say goodbye: A life of blissful simplicity is ours for the taking when we say farewell to what no longer serves us. Whether a material possession, occupation, relationship, location, or even a state-of-mind, letting go allows us unlimited space for creating the life of our dreams. Ideas and opportunities take flight when we lighten our load. Just how far will you be able to fly without your feet tethered to the floor?

Abandon the affluent mindset: If you truly desire the simple life, then get back to the basics: food, clothing, shelter, and connection to others. Determine your needs from your wants and make a plan to reduce the burdens you've been shouldering. Eliminate your debts, sell or donate your unwanted stuff, and consolidate into a smaller living space. Do you need a car? With fewer bills to pay, a smaller number of rooms to maintain, and more time in your life, you just may discover YOU.

Eliminate excessive activities: No need to fill your schedule with things that don't truly resonate, just because you feel you should be doing them. Why make your children take piano lessons if they prefer only karate? Allow someone else to run the book club if you find it a bore. Things will still function in the office if you aren't the one volunteering for extra projects. Cut back and learn to enjoy some down time.

Find a simple twin: You'll find it easier to give up things and develop a new way of being if you have the support of a good friend. Form a simplicity partnership and help each other look for ways you can make positive shifts. We are often blind to what is right in front of us. A good friend will be honest and aware of ways you can simplify. Not only is it nice to have a fresh set of eyes on a problem, you'll also benefit from the emotional embrace from someone you love.

Write your final wishes: Sit down with conscious awareness and reflect on your past, your present, and the intentions you'd like to set for the future. What do you love about your life? What has worked? What hasn't? Think about the legacy you wish to leave for others. What would you be known for? Your smile, generous spirit, or maybe the way you lovingly cared for children? If your life isn't what you have envision for yourself, honor that too and begin making changes *today*. It is never too late. We are always, in every moment, shaping our lives.

Ignition points

- Do something fun in honor of a departed loved one. Have that person's favorite meal or take a drive to a place dear to your loved one's heart. Can you feel their love?
- Eliminate the multiples in your life. Do you need thirty pairs of shoes or boxes of old jewelry and accessories? Make an investment in a few quality pieces and let the others go.

Chapter Six Exercise – Ignite CALM

Time to simply be

Timeline Exercise

In this exercise, you will take stock of your timeline for an average day and an average week. Don't try this with an unusual week, such as a vacation away from home or when you're working against a tight deadline. Let's examine a typical day and week in your life.

To begin this exercise, write a weekly schedule on a sheet of paper or use a pre-printed weekly calendar. The dates are not as important as the days of the week, Sunday through Saturday, a seven-day period.

For each day of the week, establish a twenty-four hour clock. We all have 168 hours each week to spend just as we would use currency. How do you spend your hours? Going day by day fill each day's clock with the following blocks and the amount of time required:

Sleep time
Work time
Family time
My time.

If you like working with colors, use markers or highlighters to show each block in a different color, so you can quickly see the distinct blocks. We will categorize every moment of each day of the week. No time period can be left without an assignment to one of our blocks. Be honest with yourself on how much time is allocated for each effort, so you can clearly see where your time is spent.

If your eight-hour workday also involves a two-hour commute, make sure to put those 10 hours into your work block. In this exercise, only categorize something as "Work time," if you're paid money for your efforts and are required to be there. This block is for your formal profession. We work all the time in life, so examine what category that work should be in and who it is in service to. Any work as a volunteer should be scheduled as "My time," because it isn't mandatory and is time you're donating for a cause you care about.

Any activities in support of your family, such as travel to and from school, sporting events, and grocery shopping should be in the family block. "Sleep time" is the period from turning out the light, putting your head on the pillow through the moment you wake up to your alarm clock in the morning. It should also include naps during the day. Waking hours at home need to be categorized as either "Family time" or "My time" depending on what you're doing. If your kids are self-sufficient and get themselves up and out each day, label the time as "My time." The same for social networking and watching TV. "Family time" is only for time you are interacting or actively in service to your family.

Go through this process for all seven days. Hopefully you will have some variations on your days off from work. Look closely at your schedule. Is it what you thought it would be? Do you have more "My time" than you expected, or less? Are you getting enough sleep to be healthy? Are you working too much, or not enough? How would you like to spend this currency of time differently?

Look at the intersection points of the blocks, where our "family time" meets "work time." If you were to make changes, how would your ideal schedule look? How can you simplify your life and calendar to make more time for what you value? Be honest with yourself about whether or not you're making the most of your time. Are you wasting your "My time" by zoning out being bored, but you crave more free time to go out with friends to have fun? Can you do anything to change that?

Set your schedule aside for a few weeks, then go back and look at it again. Did your knowledge of the time blocks change your behavior over the past week or so? If you were to update your schedule what would have changed? Knowing you are consciously creating your life in each and every moment, what changes do you wish to implement over time to improve the quality of life for you and your family?

Keep in mind, there is no ideal ratio of the time blocks that equal a life of happiness. We all like different things. If working a dozen hours a day feeds your soul, then go for it. Each of us with unique interests, values, and goals has the freedom to design the life we desire.

Make a priority to carve out time to simply be. Decades from now we will not be depressed wishing we'd spent more time in traffic or farming cyber radishes on a computer game. Can you see the potential of creating a life in which your time blocks blend in beautiful harmony? Your work supporting your family gives rise to contentment and a happy you, who is getting a blissful night's sleep ready to do it all again in the morning. Sweet dreams.

Chapter Seven
Money & Abundance

"Too many people spend money they haven't earned, to buy things they don't want, to impress people that they don't like."
—Will Rogers

MONEY, ALTHOUGH A SIMPLE INSTRUMENT, has become a complicated game in our society. In its original and purest form, money is a tool—a way to efficiently exchange our energy, time, and efforts for things we value and need. You may be surprised to know that I enjoy cash as much as the next person and like having the opportunity to give and receive money freely. What I don't like is the idea of money being the controlling factor in life.

It's tragic to see talented, loving people throw away their true riches of time and relationships in pursuit of a pot of gold. There's solid reason money is referred to as "cold, hard cash," because it will not hold you close, warm your heart, or listen intently as you discuss your hopes and dreams.

My goal for you in writing this chapter is to take the sting out of money and allow a healthy relationship to develop between you and money. When you look at your connection to currency as an evolving and ever-changing pathway in the course of an entire lifetime, you will see where your opportunities truly lie and where they do not.

As with anything in our world, there is no one path to financial riches. That would be impossible, because each of us has a unique perspective, background, experience, and energy signatures that create different outcomes. I imagine a few "get rich quick" salespeople will roll their eyes at me while reading this; people who believe their formula is the right way for everyone and the only way. Yes, you'll encounter people who recommend ways to make sure bets in your financial life, but never forget to add the most important ingredient to the recipe—you.

Once we escape the stranglehold of money's power, we allow ourselves to live life more vibrantly, without concern. We control the money, instead of money controlling us. Without attachment, we are able to make decisions with clarity without being distracted by the passions of an addictive monetary love affair.

In the chapter on simplicity I discussed a few ways to make things easier by lessening our dependence on cash and changing how we live day-to-day. By simplifying, we can separate our wants from our needs and clearly determine exactly what we value in life. Do you find your relationships and time more valuable than money? If so, how can you make decisions to best support that? If not, why is money more important than your peace of mind and time with your family and friends? Money can never replace the connections we have to our higher self or our relationship to another soul.

My client Jonah, a kind man and a hard worker, was myopic in pursuit of wealth. He envisioned being a millionaire before age forty, which in his mind would then deliver him a beautiful wife, talented children, and great happiness. His challenge? He was blind to life happening around him as he attempted to create a financial legacy. Wearing a Rolex, driving around in a Mercedes, and working eighty hours a week to try and keep up with his own image of wealth, he didn't give himself time to truly connect with people. He was lonely. The women he met were attracted to the flash of his cash and had little substance for discussing the art and philosophy he also had passion for.

"They are so shallow," he would say to me in session after another break-up that predictably happened when a woman realized the amount of work and significant debt that also came with the relationship. Jonah had a difficult time seeing he was getting what he was asking for, someone just as caught up in money as he was. Within a single year Jonah was laid off from his job, his investments took a nosedive with the economy, and he lost many of his properties. Being stripped of the false foundations allowed him to do inner work and determine what truly mattered to him, beyond the bucks. Only after losing all of his money did he finally realize what little value it held in his world.

Jonah is a perfect example of someone with a great work ethic who paid little attention to his soul's urgings. He was conflicted because what he worked so hard to achieve was not giving him the happiness it promised. We are programmed in our society to go after money with gusto, to use numbers as a measure of self-value whether it is in the form of a paycheck, stock portfolio, or even our weight on the bathroom scale in the morning. We can avoid repeating Jonah's misstep by being conscious of our authentic needs and ignoring the false promises and characteristics we think will come with financial wealth. It is time we are measured by the benevolence in our hearts and the supportive nature of our actions. What are we doing to make the world a better place? When Jonah took his addiction to money out of the happiness equation, he was able to create a life in greater alignment with his soul. He has dominion over money, instead of being a slave to it, and he can now attract situations and relationships in which he is valued for being who he is.

When the law of attraction doesn't work

A number of years ago when the "law of attraction" books and classes began to take center stage I noticed a great number of people misinterpreting the information, trying to use it as a gateway to fame and wealth. Instead of understanding the provocative lessons on thought and action that were being presented, many people grabbed onto the sales pitch while ignoring the philosophical concepts. People were trying to create magic with only a portion of the potion and then were angry when it didn't work. That's too bad, because this model and the teachings are valuable when properly understood and implemented.

What concerned me was the number of people who believed by "acting" and spending as if they were already wealthy, they would manifest greater riches and eventually cover their financial outlay. Uh-oh! You can see how this could get people into trouble fast if they allowed their egos to spin tales and professed a reality that didn't truly exist. Here's the rub about misrepresentation, also based on the law of attraction: If you lie, you will attract more lies and deception into your personal orbit. You will keep wealth and abundance at arm's reach by focusing your attention on lack, falsehoods, and facades.

By being honest and accepting reality wherever we are, financially, physically, and emotionally, we tame our fickle egos and allow room for positive dreams and intentions to take root and grow. We have faith that our thoughts and actions will manifest our wishes. You won't grow a watermelon with a pumpkin seed, no matter what you believe. But you can use your resources to grow the best darn pumpkin of the season. By letting go of our *sole* projection of how something should be within our limited perception, we are leaving room for the *soul* possibilities, which are limitless.

> *"Wealth consists not in having great possessions,*
> *but in having few wants."*
> —Epictetus

Tell me what you want. C'mon, what is it you truly desire in this world? Who do you wish to be? When we absolutely know what we want and can hone in on it, then we're able to create it. Abundance in all forms will flow to us in support of our efforts.

Also understand we can be compensated with things that are more valuable than money—the proverbial "things money can't buy." How is the Universe paying you? Your riches may come in the form of friends, family, love, joy, health, or flower gardens. Maybe your abundance is in the ideas you have or the opportunities you can't see because you're too busy looking the other way. I challenge you to take stock of what you have. Quiet the negative mind and gather your courage to take actions on your inspirations. Often the only difference between a frustrated worker and the person living her dreams is doing inner work and taking the leap with confidence.

The manifestation of this book is a great example of how anyone can follow the energy of a situation, seize the moment, and create abundance. Yes, I mean you! As you may recall from Chapter One, I was inspired by a negative situation to make positive changes for myself and for others. On some cosmic level the book's time had come. The idea grew wings and is now taking flight. I signed with my publisher within a week of submitting my proposal, because it resonated strongly for everyone involved. Finding a publisher is rarely that easy. Trust me, I have faced my share of rejections as an author, even shelving a few projects over the past few years because I couldn't get energy or support from others. Like many writers, I have files of ideas and research awaiting their day in the sun. The important point is, I always kept at it.

At this moment in time, the book's success is measurable in many ways, but no money in the bank so far. The project is still under construction. Authoring a book is an investment of time, energy, skill, and intention with great faith it will one day pay off in countless forms, including money, clients, good feelings, opportunities, accolades, invitations, or even watermelons and pumpkins. (I don't know a person in rural Maine who hasn't accepted the bounty of produce as payment at one point or another).

So here I am, sitting barefoot at my laptop, investing in my future, snacking on salad grown in a client's garden, and chatting with my husband about how to keep our expenses down until the money flow goes up again. It's all perfect, because this profession allows me to be true to myself and the benefits of freedom are worth more than compromising my principles.

What dream in your heart are you working for? Not all work has a steady or robust payday. In some callings it's never about the money— the best dividends come from the peace and satisfaction of a job well done, or meaningful labor in service to others.

> *"No matter how rich you become, how famous or powerful, when you die the size of your funeral will still pretty much depend on the weather."*
> —Michael Pritchard

World famous billionaire investor Warren Buffet is known for his belief in simple living and frugality. Although he's one of the richest men in the world and could do anything with his vast wealth, he chooses a life of simplicity and has pledged to donate 99 percent of his fortune to philanthropic causes during the course of his lifetime, or upon his death. Living in the same modest home he purchased over fifty years ago in Omaha, he prefers a life surrounded by basic comforts without the burdens associated with keeping up the toy inventory others flaunt. His vast fortune is a powerful tool for good in the world. Warren Buffet is a happy man at work and at home because he understands that being true to his own nature and values is his greatest reward.

Research done at Princeton University in 2010 by Kahneman and Deaton[16] looked at whether income has an effect on our happiness. They examined two specific aspects of subjective well-being.

The first was *emotional well-being*, referring to "the emotional quality of an individual's everyday experience—the frequency and intensity of experiences of joy, stress, sadness, anger, and affection that make one's life pleasant or unpleasant."

The second part of well-being they examined was *life evaluation*, referring to "the thoughts people have about their life when they think about it."

---

16 "High income improves evaluation of life but not emotional well-being," Daniel Kahneman and Angus Deaton, Center for Health and Well-being, Princeton University, August 4, 2010

After examining more than 450,000 survey responses, they found emotional well-being and life evaluation correlate differently. The study revealed that having a high income improves how we evaluate our lives, but does not improve our actual emotional well-being. Interestingly, although both forms of well-being initially increased as income rose, it did not progress beyond an annual income of $75,000. The researchers concluded that high income buys life satisfaction, our perception of how we should feel about our lives, but not happiness itself. Basically, the average person looked at the physical components of their life—the things and relationships they have—and judged they *should be* satisfied with what they have, even though they were not. We think having the best toys on the block should provide happiness, but having a full garage doesn't correlate to a joyful heart. You are no happier with more money and certainly don't need to be a millionaire to increase your joy.

This study got me thinking ... if money only affects our thoughts or our judgments of happiness and not *actual* happiness, what if we learn to change how we think about money? Yes, we can adjust our thoughts, regardless of the amount of money involved. Doing so is a matter of learning another way of seeing value, without being a slave to conventional thought processes and bad habits adopted through fear of lack. You can begin by using a different unit of measure to evaluate your life and evaluate its value. Perhaps our CALM components: creativity, authenticity luminosity, and mindfulness can be your new currency, or you may choose any other philosophy or idea that resonates.

This is a great blessing of our world—we each decide what's precious to us. Is it time or love? Imagine the life you'd live if you measured success by the number of smiles you created, how true you are to self, or the number of people you assist in a day. We know that doing good deeds is good for us. Allow us to accept how goodness can cause not only our perceived well-being, but also our actual well-being, to skyrocket. I don't know about you, but I'll take actual happiness over fickle fear-based perceptions any day of the week!

Time to light up the topic of money. What is your relationship to money at this point in your life? Does it frighten you or invigorate you? Take a moment to review the chart below to see how we can ignite CALM in how we relate to money and attract abundance in our lives:

	Ignite CALM for Money & Abundance
Creativity:	Have I looked at the issue of money and abundance creatively?
Authenticity:	Am I being true to my personal values and goals in my effort to make money in this manner?
Luminosity:	Am I bringing the best of me to this issue of making money and creating abundance?
Mindfulness:	How does my relationship to and decisions about money and abundance affect my life and others?

This straightforward technique can help you evaluate investments, decide on career changes, make major purchases, and determine savings. Remember this method is simple, yet profound, because you must go deep within yourself for the answers. The values held by your soul rise to the surface when you look through this high vibration filter, leaving your fears and the projections of others behind. This method puts you front and center, because YOU are the central point we're focusing on. This is your life. By concentrating on your heart's desire and beginning to chart your course, you best serve everyone else in your life.

It doesn't matter whether or not you've figured out *how to do something*. What matters is that you're beginning to learn *what you want to do*. You'll be amazed at how the Universe will assist you, once you determine what you want. Why stay in limbo? Your happiness is worth the effort. Here are a few ideas on igniting the fire of abundance in your life:

Ignite Abundance

Don't sell yourself short: In our fast-paced, crazy lives, it's crucial that we understand and appreciate our own value. Your job may think your rate is $15 per hour, but to your loved ones your time with them is priceless. Make your decisions with the currency of all your values in mind. If you jokingly state you would pay yourself to NOT do something, then don't do it. Appreciate your worth and the worth of those around you.

Don't fear change: We can get shaken up when we realize things we've relied on are about to make a sudden shift. Companies close or make cutbacks, spouses become ill and cannot work, or a natural disaster requires us to move. All these things rock our worlds and we must find a way to cope. And we always do. Change is a constant force we all deal with. Have faith in yourself. You will be able to navigate these transformations with grace.

Don't mistake cost for value: At any given moment in our lives, we're bombarded by sales pitches in the form of, signs, commercials, phone calls, emails, and Tweets about how we need to become smart, sexy, and popular. With subtle seduction these sales tactics brainwash us into thinking we'll be better, and happier, if our possessions are numerous and cost more. Don't fall for marketing. The value of a person is best measured in their heart's intention, demonstrated through behavior, choices, and actions.

Don't limit potential: You do yourself and others a tremendous disservice by constructing strict boundaries to growth and possibility. Dare to dream and lend your positive energy to others who want to strive for more. Whether it's running a marathon, launching a new business, auditioning for a role in a movie, or enrolling in medical school, take a chance on your desires and help others do the same. So much is out there waiting for you.

Don't covet thy neighbor's anything: If you see something you desire over the fence, then have the courage to craft it for yourself. Comparing our lives to others and feeling we're always on the short end is a vast misunderstanding based on the lowest energy commodity—stuff. Look a little deeper and ask yourself why you crave a particular item or situation. If the desire is worthy and legitimate, then take down the barriers you've built to having it in your own life. Wanting will only breed more want—manifest instead.

Don't build your wealth from loss: Other people's misfortune should not be to your advantage. To benefit from the pain or loss of others is not only malicious and inhuman, but also an invitation for another to victimize you. "What comes around goes around," and you need not create the karma of breaking the Golden Rule. Energetic balance is exact and swift. Be the person who helps others in all walks of life.

Expand your skills: We create greater opportunities for abundance and wealth when our talents and abilities allow us to serve others in society. We need one another to create communities of diversity and skill. Artists, doctors, machinists, police officers, teachers, cleaners, and so on ... we're all needed to make this world work. If you don't like the job you're doing, learn to do something else.

Make the world your classroom: Take the time and energy to invest in your life by creating opportunities for growth and adventure. You can learn as much in acts of daily living as you would in any classroom. Make the world your school by surrounding yourself with new people and experiences. Allow the Universe to introduce you to innovative prospects and possibilities that exist around every corner. Experience is priceless!

Know when to splurge: Say yes to something you truly desire in recognition of all you do. You've earned it and should celebrate. There are times in our lives when we need to indulge in a gift or an extravagant meal for the pure enjoyment of living. If we splurge all the time, then the occasion loses importance and becomes just another mindless bad habit of pleasing our egos. Take your daily rewards in positive feelings, but also know when to party!

Understand where you stand: We're most empowered financially when we clearly understanding the facts of our situation. Pretending money doesn't exist or matter at all will not help you pay the bills every month. Money is essential in our society for exchanging goods and services. Knowing what's coming in and going out allows us to make educated and precise decisions on how we live each moment. Only we can forge our path to fiscal freedom.

Know your needs: Mistaking wants for needs is a bad habit we've all found ourselves getting into. Do we *need* cable TV, the latest cell phone, or another car? Perhaps we do, or perhaps we don't. Take inventory of your basics and your extras. You don't need to eliminate things you want as long as you're honest with yourself they are luxuries, not needs. Why burden yourself with the stress of a $100,000 job when your needs could be nicely met earning a fraction of that? The choice is always yours.

Embrace flux: One person's stress is another's adventure. Opening our hearts to the vast fluctuations of life can open the door to greater wealth and abundance. Employers often reward those who are willing to take a chance in service to the company. Seriously consider agreeing to the relocation offer or accepting a promotion. There's a reason the opportunity was given to you and not another. Pay close attention to how change may benefit you.

Ignition points

- Simplify your charitable giving by selecting a few charities close to your heart and supporting them fully through volunteering, spreading awareness, and yes, cash if you have it to give.
- Reduce your stress by affordably consolidating revolving debt. Receiving only one bill every month is easier to manage and will help you keep track of your true expenses and goals to eliminate the debt altogether.

Chapter Seven Exercise – Ignite CALM

What it's worth

In this exercise you're going to have fun thinking of things you'd like to bring into your life, including material items, experiences, emotions, and sensations. We'll be looking at "cost" and "worth" in a new way. You'll need a pen, a piece of paper, and maybe a calculator, if you don't want to get a brain cramp. This exercise will take 15 to 30 minutes to complete. Here's your opportunity to dream big and be specific about what you want in life.

If there were no limits, what would you want?
Is it a fancy sports car? If so, what year and model?
Is it a relationship? What kind?
An emotion? Describe it.
A great new job? Be specific.

Perhaps a trip around the world, a skydiving adventure, or maybe a fabulous new home is on your list. Begin thinking without restriction or judgment of yourself. After pondering for a few moments, begin making a list in a column of what you want. Write as many items on the list as you like, making sure you have at least ten things.

Next, write your best estimate for the monetary value of each item. It doesn't have to be exactly to the penny, but use an accurate representation of the item's cash value. Is that car worth $30,000 or $130,000? If you don't have a good idea of a financial value, then perform a quick Internet search to find it. If you think your item doesn't have a monetary cost, then place a zero for value. Often things that cost nothing pay us in happiness and positive experiences.

Now, go back to your list and write beside each item what it represents to you emotionally. How do you feel when you think about that item? For example, why does that particular car matter to you? Does it represent freedom? Or joy? Or security? Decide why you want it. Do this for each entry on the list. Figure out why it strikes your fancy.

We are going to calculate your hourly adjusted rate the CALM way, and we'll include all your time in a given week, because time is valuable. We are NOT only using the hours you get paid to do work.

1. If you earn $800 per week, divide that by 168 hours, because that's how many hours you live in a week. Your rate would be $4.76 per hour.
2. Write your hourly pay rate in the upper right hand corner of the page.
3. Having established your hourly rate, divide each of your desired items by your CALM adjusted hourly rate and write the number beside it. If your car was valued at $30,000, then you will write 6302 hours (30,000 divided by 4.76 is 6302). At this point in time, you understand the car is worth $30,000 and 6302 hours of your time. This is how much time out of your life the car will cost you. Do this for every item on the list. Now you can see the currency of both money and time.
4. Write the number 655,200 on your page. This is your lifetime budget of hours, if you live to be 75 years old. One by one, subtract the time cost of each item on your list. When you get to the zero valued items, give yourself a +100,000 bonus for items that have no cost. You are actually adding hours for those, not taking away. (I told you they paid in the long run!)

When you finish doing the math, what are you left with? Did you run out of time or have plenty to spare? What if your potential were more than your time and wage?

Here's a little magic. **Anything and everything is possible and can shift in a moment.** Any desire or item that may seem out of your grasp can miraculously be yours. Do you remember how I made $50,000 in ten minutes on the domain name sale? What about when the charity also received a generous donation of a magazine to publish, seemingly out of the blue?

This is the place where anything is possible if we are open to the beauty and power of the Universe working through us. A windfall in any form already exists for each and every one of us. We need only place ourselves in the proper vibration and state of manifestation to follow the whispers, inspirations ... and do the work!

Reflect upon this entire exercise, looking at time, money and miracles as all things available to you to create the life of your dreams!

Chapter Eight
Carrying the Torch of Leadership

> *"As we look ahead into the next century, leaders will be those who empower others."*
> —Bill Gates

WHEN WE HAVE CONSCIOUS leaders lighting the way, there will be no limit to the greatness our society can experience. This is what the elements of CALM point to: being conscious, acutely aware of, and concerned about our world and the people in it. When we ignite CALM, we are making an active choice to bring the best of ourselves to whatever we do in the present moment. This extends to all areas of our lives; at home, in our work and also our relationships to those we care about.

Imagine how wonderful it would be to work with a leader who not only embraces these philosophies, but also demonstrates them in all aspects of life.

Can you be that leader?

Unfortunately, most of us have suffered at the hands of poor leadership. We've had to work with people who are the opposite of what we strive for with CALM. Narcissistic, power hungry bullies often gain favor in the workplace because their ruthless techniques save companies money. We see reality television shows featuring business leaders as "sharks" or egomaniacal jerks who care about nothing beside the bottom line, or demonstrating their control over others through threats and manipulation.

Enough already! Our world should no longer emulate or honor people who only work toward their own selfish gains in business, politics, celebrity circles, sports, or even in families. It's time we stand up for goodness, sending the corrupt tormenters on their way. Let us learn from the rise and fall of men like Bernie Madoff and the Enron moguls, whose actions, devoid of a moral compass, led to their own destruction.

Years ago I attended a training meeting in which one of the junior managers was trying to make an impression on higher ups by bringing the other forty people on the team to task. He paced the room fuming and fussing like a spoiled child, throwing out insulting barbs to people and making many people cringe in fear. Several of us, instead of getting fearful, got frustrated. Okay, we were pissed. We began to set our jaws and shifting our bodies to form a protective shield against his angry speech. I took notes and waited for an appropriate moment to raise my hand and ask a question.

"What, Deb, what?" he bellowed upon seeing my hand.

I said, "Do you actually think this entire group of people wants to get it all wrong? Perhaps if we focused on learning the proper methods, we could accomplish something."

Several others in the group immediately voiced agreement. The man detested me at that moment, his laser eyes burning through me. Not knowing how to respond to the team pushing back, he stared at us in shock. His boss quickly stood and moved the meeting along, wrapping up the issue by stating, "A memo will be released with the revised protocol. Please review it."

For the rest of the day I received smiles and thank you messages from my colleagues. We were all tired of being battered. We stood together for fairness and our collective voice was heard.

Harassment and bullying take many forms. Years ago when I worked in radio broadcasting, I was sexually harassed many times by more than one person in the fast paced party-like atmosphere. I never filed complaints, making light of these situations in fear of losing my job. Over twenty-five years later, I see I let myself down and did a disservice to other women at the station by being silent. At that time of my young life, I didn't value myself enough to speak out against the sexual harassment. Abusers get away with their abhorrent behavior because on some level we allow them to. We're afraid to make the situation worse by drawing attention to ourselves, because we fear being punished or blamed. It is important we understand and defend the principle that no one has the right to treat another in an unkind and unfair way. No one. No parent, boss, teacher, coach, director, or any co-worker should feel it's their place to belittle another person. Our roles may be different, yet our souls are equal.

No one should fear a boss and certainly no one should be forced to act outside their own principles. There will always be another job. Work that goes against our grain will take its toll on our health, happiness, and sense of worth.

Leaders must rise to each occasion, energetically altering their conduct, being mindful, flexible, and always protecting those they are responsible for in every situation. Although we can all relate to being annoyed if someone in our charge is making mistakes, our responsibility is to handle the circumstance in a respectable, professional manner. Haven't we all made mistakes on the job? When we allow anger and an unchecked ego to control our behavior, we're allowing the worst of us to be in charge and not the best.

Rooted in Catholicism and taught in numerous religions across our world, teachings of the Seven Cardinal Sins were created to temper behavior. They are most commonly known as: wrath, greed, sloth, pride, lust, envy, and gluttony. Each trait sounds dramatic, fierce, and frightening, and of course must only apply to the worst of the worst of people—not us. Of course not us! We must realize that every element of the seven sins was once only a mere seed, a habit that was given energy and allowed to grow into a person's everyday character until it began to define his or her behavior and life. We all carry around bags of seeds. Which ones do we sow?

Being apathetic is a seed that, if given the proper energy, allows sloth to take over. Think of this the next time you sit at a café. Pay attention to the dozens of people who ignore one another while mindlessly attending to their phones and devices. We're getting caught up in the weeds of a capitalistic, commercialized projection of life on a teeny, tiny screen, instead of life itself. Any behavior, whether virtuous or offensive, can be grown in our lives if we plant it, feed it, and allow it flourish. We choose for ourselves if our gardens are filled with stunning, colorful flowers or choking weeds.

> *"Before you are a leader, success is all about growing yourself. When you become a leader, success is all about growing others."*
> —Jack Welch

The Journal of Positive Psychology shared research in 2010[17] looking at the effects of leaders' moral excellence and how they elicit positive emotions within organizations. The researchers found that:

> "leaders' self-sacrifice and interpersonal fairness are powerful elicitors of *elevation*, known as a reaction to moral excellence and that this emotion fully mediates leaders' influence on followers' organizational citizenship behavior and affective organizational commitment."

The researchers believe these results point to the importance of positive moral emotions within organizations and give standing that leaders can foster these positive emotions and ethics, thus creating beneficial outcomes for their organizations. Put simply, if you have a fair and ethical person in a leadership role, workers respond and mirror the positive behavior. Everyone will be happier, and the company will thrive. When each person does his best in service to a common goal, everyone reaps the rewards.

---

17 Vianello, Michelangelo , Galliani, Elisa Maria and Haidt, Jonathan(2010) "Elevation at work: The effects of leaders' moral excellence," *The Journal of Positive Psychology*, 5: 5, 390- 411, http://dx.doi.org/10.1080/17439760.2010.516764.

Self-leadership

Every one of us can initiate opportunities and pave the way to find meaningful work at a job we truly love. The fun part? It's unique for each of us. We must personally take a stand for what we believe in our hearts is right for us and be the confident leader of our own lives. If we don't actively shape our world to match our positive visions of how we believe life should be, who will? Let's work together and find our passion for living and working again by creating lives we are grateful for from beginning to end, from front porch to cubicle.

Being the leader of your own life means making choices in support of your soul. Work for people you value, who will value you. Do you really think we're here to just be pawns in another person's money game? Hell no! We are here to be happy, vibrant beings on an adventure we call life. When we stop playing other people's games we can make choices that enrich us. Our lives become a force of positive, vibrant action, instead of mere survival-based reactions.

My client Sydney enjoyed her job, but was struggling financially even though she and her husband both worked full time. Having their kids in daycare took a huge chunk out of the family budget each week, and it seemed as soon as they started getting ahead, something else would crop up to steal away the savings. We can all relate to this on some level can't we? Sydney and her husband sat down, did the math, and were surprised to discover her job was actually costing them money. When they added up the expenses of childcare, travel, and meals on the go, the total amount swallowed her entire salary.

Deciding to be her own life leader, Sydney left her job to stay home with her children. Along with that decision, she and her husband chose to vastly reduce their expenses. Although she no longer gets a weekly check, she is now paid in other ways—mainly giggles and quality time with her family. Sydney made the choice to no longer work outside the home when she realized the lifestyle they had, which required two incomes, wasn't needed for their happiness. This family was able to discover new pathways to the good life by getting down to the basics of what was important to them.

I realize many of you are not in the position to change jobs right now. For one reason or another you must remain in your present occupation. So how can you make the most of it? How can you find bliss at work in your work life when things are challenging and, at times, feel soul crushing?

You begin by taking responsibility for your own happiness in all aspects of your life. And start making a plan. I don't want to call it an escape plan, or even a formula for success. Our ignite CALM action plan is to use the CALM components and questions to address the individual challenges you face and help determine what you want in life. When you have a goal and a desired outcome you'll feel better because you're working toward it every day, even if you can only take small steps at a time.

Shift how you look at work and realize it goes beyond paid employment or any one profession. Our lives are already filled with positive work and most of us by nature love to keep busy doing something. I venture to guess the average person dislikes boredom more than activity, or even hard physical labor. So this comes down to a matter of making what you do more enjoyable, or at least acceptable. We work in gardens, tinker on vehicles, hike trails, and cook meals. These activities would be fun for one person and a chore for another. It's all a matter of perspective.

We need to follow what resonates with us individually and ignites our spirit. So, if you're looking for a new career because you feel burned out on your current one, do some soul searching to find what elevates you. Are you building barriers to your own happiness by refusing to budge from where you are because you fear taking a risk on something new? What holds deep meaning in your life? Animals? Children? Being of service? Have you always wanted to be a forensic scientist?

Follow that energy. No one can stop you from creating opportunities for yourself. If someone tries to control you, make different choices in your relationships and be the one responsible for your own happiness. A fun job that pays the bills might be all you need while you advance your skills and build toward your dream career. Cooking breakfast at an antique inn at the ocean wasn't glamorous, but I loved the people I worked with and the pure satisfaction I felt at the end of every shift after feeding delicious food to dozens of hungry customers. It also financed my college education, so that was a plus.

Become the leader of your own life by calling the shots yourself. Here are tips on igniting leadership in our lives:

Ignite Leadership

Don't fear the sharks: People and experiences are put into our lives for us to learn from, so we can evolve and benefit from those encounters. Sometimes we learn from positive influences, and other times we learn by witnessing poor behavior. Life is powerful when we're aware and able to make use of our experiences. After seeing the benefits of swimming with the dolphins and the sharks, you won't be fish bait.

Don't doubt your leadership skills: If you're feeling especially challenged to step up your game by supervisors, that may be a sign it's time for you to embrace an enhanced role on the job. Take your ideas of innovation to the next level by becoming a leader yourself. When we work to develop others, we are also developing ourselves. Keep CALM in heart and mind and you will know without a doubt you will be able to light the path to achievement for you and the team.

Don't expect more than you give: Avoid the common pitfall of having your demands outweigh what you're willing to deliver. Business is business and needs to deliver top-notch products and services to customers while making a profit. If you're only working at a fraction of your skill or production level, how can you expect a favorable return? Meet your employer in the middle, being clear on your goals and expectations. A job well done delivers advantages greater than money.

Don't complain without solutions: This is how many people choose to work—and why they fail and are unhappy. Grumbling and groaning, fussing and moaning, we all know at least one person at work who cannot stop complaining. Be the person with the solution. If you identify a problem, take time to think about it and research how it might be solved. Making the attempt demonstrates your concern for the company beyond yourself.

Don't sabotage those in power: Although we may not always agree with our managers and those in charge, we should have respect for the positions they hold. Our employers, based upon their own reasoning, have determined these supervisors are worthy of the jobs they've been given. Undermining them will only have a negative effect on you. Have the integrity to express your concerns respectfully and in the open.

Don't be a lazy dog: Unless you're teaching the finer points of napping, being lazy and taking the easy way out will not earmark you for a leadership role on the job. Some people extend a great deal of energy trying to avoid work, when in reality they only attract the resentment of colleagues and exasperation from the boss. If your laziness comes from boredom, it's time to try modifications that will reinvigorate your day.

Express your truth: You know your job inside and out and you're good at it. Often called on to train your fellow teammates, you always help with extra responsibilities when needed. So why be silent when things need to be said? Your employer relies on your talents and expertise. They have invested in you over the years and welcome your unique, skilled perspective. Most companies truly want their employees to speak out with ideas, concerns, and collaborations. Go for it!

Be flexible: When given the responsibility to guide others, we should remember to be open and adaptable to the changing needs of all involved. Rigidity and self-righteousness will quickly alienate you from the people you're meant to inspire. Demonstrating flexibility allows others to see you're one of them and you do understand the diverse challenges of daily living.

Accept extra responsibility: Taking leadership in our professions and communities tells those around us that we're willing and able to accept the responsibility of carrying the torch for our colleagues, students, and friends. Not only are we handling our own work, we agree to lend our experience to others, assisting with their tasks and professional development. Exceptional leaders help create new leaders without fear of competition.

Embrace diversity: You can offer no finer gift to someone than seeing them for the unique person they are and acknowledging the good they do in this world. Understanding we each have a part to play regardless of background, race, gender, age, experience, and ability level, helps successful leaders empower those in their world to be at their best and strive for more. We all bring something different to the table. Embracing what makes others special and creating opportunities for them is a mark of someone truly great.

Know your weaknesses: We gain powerful and commanding strength when we learn to recognize our own weaknesses. Embrace what challenges you by honoring, then conquering the difficulty. Those of us who think we know it all are only demonstrating how much we have to learn.

See your life fully: We are empowered when we know we're more than any job, the roles we play in our families, or labels assigned to us. We are individuals; complex, yet simple; unique, yet ordinary—and each of us is an exceptional, crucial part of the whole. When we see our lives as opportunities to express ourselves in curious and creative ways, we leave behind the pressure of having to fit into a rigid mold someone else designed. Be the leader of your life by creating greatness in you.

Ignition points

- Inspire those around you by freely sharing truthful confessions of your own weaknesses and strengths, as well as your positive observations of their behavior. When we relate to one another as equals, we foster greater understanding within the group.
- Make an effort to be the one who lights the way for others by being true to who you are. Your life at work and at home will benefit when you are your most creative, authentic, luminous, and mindful self. Dare to ignite CALM and see bliss at work in your life!

Chapter Eight Exercise—Ignite CALM

Leading light

In this exercise, I'd like you to envision what traits you believe leaders in our society should have, and whether you personally identify yourself as a leader. This activity can be done with a pen and a piece of paper and will take about 20 minutes. Remember to be absolutely honest in your answers, because you will only benefit if you make a sincere effort.

In your mind's eye, picture your ultimate ideal leader or boss. What characteristics would this person have? If you had a favorite mentor in the past think about what you liked about that man or woman. Would those characteristics hold up for you now?

Make a list of the leadership traits for your ideal. Use details about this person's looks, actions, age, education, background, manner of speech, and how they relate to others on their teams. List all the things you respect and find important in a leader.

Consider all the different roles leaders hold in our world. They can be teachers, coaches, politicians, managers, business owners, or directors of charities and organizations. Thinking of the many faces of leadership will help you complete your list, especially if you feel stuck on what to write.

Now, look over your list of leadership qualities. Do any of the attributes you recorded fall within our CALM components? Write beside each item on your list whether it aligns with Creativity, Authenticity, Luminosity or Mindfulness. If it is suitable for more than one of those categories, list all it corresponds with. For example, if you wrote your leader should be a passionate, confident speaker, you might want to mark that as fitting into Creativity and also Authenticity. It's all up to you. This is the boss of your dreams and you're the best person to flesh it out. If an attribute doesn't correspond with our CALM components, circle the listed item so your can remember to individually assess it.

Review the list of characteristics and what CALM components they may fall into. Do you see any patterns? What can those circled traits tell you about the boss you most desire to work with? Do you desire a boss who is creative? Perhaps authenticity is most important to you. Is your ideal boss all business, or do you prefer a more casual, relatable style?

How does your ideal match up with bosses and leaders you have in your life now? Could anyone in this world rise to the occasion and be this type of boss? Are your projections for the leader realistic and reasonable?

Now look at your own potential for leadership based upon the characteristics you consider essential. Do you see yourself in this description? Could you be this boss if you wanted to be? If you applied it to yourself, would you add or take away and items on your list? Think about your life and examine why you're making the choice to be a leader or not be a leader at this point in time. Do you believe you can be a successful leader?

Here is a magnificent opportunity to improve your work and home life by helping your boss become a better leader. How are you as a follower? Be honest about whether or not you're a good team player and do your fair share. Are you one to support the commander or do you speak ill behind his back? Can you learn to support people around you who accept the added responsibilities of leadership?

If you want a boss with fantastic communication skills and you don't currently have one, then you've identified an area that can be improved. Now use your own fabulous communication skills to do something about it. Whether you stuff the department's suggestion box, use the information as talking points during a team meeting, or bring it up with Human Resources, you can work on finding an appropriate solution to this challenge. Just remember to offer your skills without insulting your boss.

Be the problem solver, not the complainer. One of my favorite bosses, a vice-president at an insurance company, refused to hear complaints from his staff unless they also had a proposed solution to the difficulty. That policy kept ideas high and fruitless complaints low. A smart, kind man, he left a positive impression on me by being a conscious leader with a strong degree of humanity and integrity.

Chapter Nine
Conscious Collaboration

Thank you for being courageous enough to accept my call to action to "Ignite CALM" and light your own inner fire. By accessing this sacred place within yourself, you have looked at your life through a high vibration filter and can now make positive, conscious choices in support of your spirit.

Where we work, what we do, and how we do it—the power is all in our own capable hands. All things we experience are intimately connected; every action we take, every decision we make, brings us further from or closer to the wishes of our souls.

We must release the shackles placed upon us by insecurity and see beyond the narrow focus of others. When we are in resonance with our souls' purpose and inner calling we do not doubt our thoughts and actions. We are confident workers and can tune out the static and confusion caused by the rules and projections of others. We hear the inner voice loud and clear.

You welcome happiness by opening your heart and mind to alternative ways of thinking and taking conscious time to process your feelings. You will allow bliss to work in your life.

Enjoy this fiery process of coming alive with a new perspective, discovering your purpose in your work and other aspects of your life.

We will always be a work in progress; sometimes messy, sometimes chaotic, yet always worth the effort. Be gentle with yourself.

As you continue the journey of working with this CALM approach, give yourself full permission to explore and make mistakes as you manifest a job you love and create the life you truly desire to live. By engaging in this process of personal growth and transformation, you have proven you have the strength to unlock the gateway to your own wisdom. Now is the time to take action.

Light it up. Be yourself, without apology, in all your vibrant glory. Ignite CALM and be happy.

CALM Conscious Collaboration Exercises

For this final section of the book, I asked for contributions from a dozen different talented holistic practitioners and self-development experts. These friends and colleagues have brought forth inspirational and illuminating information and activities that help you ignite CALM in your life every day. Their unique perspectives are designed to connect with you heart to heart, giving you the opportunity to try on a variety of methods.

Bringing these experts together has created something that includes the positive energy and intention of many people, coming together to inspire. You will now join us by adding your own special energy as you complete the lessons. We are all conscious collaborators making a positive choice to shift. This gifted group of contributing writers is compromised of artists, best selling authors, teachers, dancers, yogis, shamans, and energy practitioners, among others. May their diverse perspectives get you fired up to see the opportunities inherent in CALM when you allow your own spirit to explore and express it individually.

The exercises are organized within our CALM components: Creativity, Authenticity, Luminosity, and Mindfulness. Feel free to undertake these activities in any order you see fit. Remember, this is all about *you* and your journey of happiness and wholeness. Aim for what resonates with you on any given day, and then go for it.

As with the CALM exercises I have written, these contributed explorations may be done alone or with a group of people. They make wonderful suggestions for team building projects on the job or in the classroom. Just think of the power, energy, and Light you could create if your group consciously collaborates to ignite CALM. Fire it up, friends!

Creativity Exercises

Unblocking Your Creativity
by *David B. Goldstein*

Acting creativity helps to solve problems—and also helps us become more engaged with our work and more fulfilled in our lives. But, accessing our creativity doesn't always happen on demand. Sometimes we block our own ideas and actions.

What many people haven't considered about creativity is that we're all creative in our own ways and the best way to gain access and understand your own style is to know more about your own personality. There are many reasons we get blocked, and different personalities each have their individual obstacles. Knowing yourself and recognizing your obstacles is the first step to overcoming them.

While there are many aspects of our personalities, knowing about one particular part is the key to getting unblocked. Doing one exercise and answering the following simple question will help get your creativity flowing.

Do you prefer to project an image of yourself and create an environment that is ordered, structured, and punctual? Or do you prefer to project an image that is spontaneous, scattered, and doing things on your own time?

We all tend to prefer one over the other most of the time. Both types of people are creative, but each type will use a different remedy to get going again when they're stuck. In fact, when we ramp up to solve a problem, too much of our own personality strengths are actually the very forces that get us stuck—so we need to temporarily reach toward our non-preferences.

If you happen to be an ordered and structured type of person, you tend to get stuck by limiting your choices and painting yourself into a corner. To break free, try something that opens you up to new ideas. Do something out of character, like having a conversation with someone you know will be a waste of time. Try reading the most uninteresting article on a topic far outside your regular pursuits. What you consider most pointless is what will challenge your assumptions and bring you the most openness to restart your creativity.

If, instead, you're the type of person who prefers to be spontaneous and do things in your own time, then opening up to new ideas is the last thing you need in order to become unblocked. In fact, too many directions leave you stuck at the crossroads, because you tend to be so open that the sheer number of possibilities can overwhelm you. To regain your traction and get going, the best medicine is to temporarily set limits, prioritize your goals, and make some tentative decisions.

Knowing this one aspect about your personality can help you find the right cure for blocked creativity. This exercise is just the beginning of how learning of your personality type can help you be more creative in your own way and gain confidence in your abilities.

The Power of Creativity
by *Jennifer Crews*

Ahhhhhhhh... the concept of creating. That's why you are here. You are meant to create. It is innately built into every fiber of your being. Every word you say, everything you do, your thoughts, your actions are all a part of the creation of You and of You creating.

Creativity is a force. A force inspired by both the physical and spiritual aspects of your environment—where your inner self lights up with an idea, a feeling, or a sense that is ready to be expressed and shared with the outer physical world. Everything you wear, say, share, write, draw, make for dinner, color, build, develop, is YOU creating.

Creativity is your inner world joining the outer world.

Take a close look around you right now. Every object you see has been created by someone. Everything, absolutely everything started as a mere spark in someone's inner world. There isn't a single item in your current surroundings whether you are at home, at work, at a coffee shop, or sitting on a park bench reading this book, that didn't start as an intricate part of someone's inner world, or the world of our ultimate Creator.

You create and even share your inner world by what color you choose to wear each day. This is you creating a mood, a look, a feel, and expression of the self. The jewelry you put on is you creating an outward expression of you. What you make yourself for breakfast is also creating; you are sharing and bringing to fruition what's inside you into the physical outside world. You like bananas on your cereal—you choose bananas and you take action and create your morning dining experience.

Even the words you speak are a form of creating. Listen to the words your co-workers use to express themselves. Listen to your friends and partners. They are creating a painting with their words on the blank canvas of space between people. Listen to the words you use to explain, describe, and share with others. Did you realize you were creating a dialogue masterpiece in every conversation?

Whether you're creating with your hands, your words, your feet, or your body, you are always sharing and bringing into the physical outside world that which is inside of you. Your unique inner self and inner world meets the physical outside world. This is all quite magical.

So you see, you're already creating each and every day from the moment you awaken, and even before, because your dreams are also creative. Creativity is not something you have to develop or go somewhere to get. It's already inside you. That is the power of creativity.

As you begin to notice more and more that every action, word, and choice you make is *you* creating, you will begin to feel the true power behind the force that is CREATIVITY.

Whether it's the simple creation of making your lunch or the more complex creation of developing a new software system to manage a company's inventory, both are equally valuable, equally important, and are equally you CREATING!

The power in knowing you create *every day* is a beautiful and freeing place to be. It gives you permission to create a masterpiece of life at your work place, at home, and everywhere you go. I remember when I first began recognizing the power of creativity. I used to own an old brown corduroy jacket I wore to work in the winter. I thought the jacket boring and dull, but it was also warm. One day I was inspired to add a sparkly pin to the collar while getting ready for work. I love jewelry and wear it all the time. My inner self always smiles when I wear something sparkly. Several of my co-workers noticed the pin and commented about how nice it looked on the jacket. This inspired me and I soon found myself sewing lace to the pockets, ribbon to the trim, and added a few more pins. Voila! I had created a brand-new looking jacket. Through the inspired creativity of sprucing up a simple jacket, I shared my inner world of loving sparkles and jewelry with the outer world. One morning I was getting a chai latte in a bustling coffee shop when the barista shouted across the counter in front of a full line of people, "Love your jacket!"

"Thanks" I responded.

"It looks great!" he replied.

To me, he was responding to more than the jacket—he liked the fact that I'd expressed my inner self and brought my individuality into the physical world. He could sense this and felt drawn to it. Other people are drawn to the "feeling" of seeing someone express their inner nature. Though they may be completely unaware, people feel it, want it for themselves, and see it in others. This is why it's so important to be open to your creative inspirations and share them with others. People will be drawn to authentic creative sharing.

Several years ago I worked for a corporate beauty company. I shared an office with four other women, and even though it was a "beauty" company, we sat at dark colored desks and were required to wear black clothing. One day during lunch I desperately wanted to brighten things up, so I bought colorful flowers for everyone for their desks. Very simple: a single flower per desk. But that simple inspiration created a significant difference in my co-workers. I had arranged the flowers on their desks just before an important meeting. Their change in attitude and productivity during the meeting was incredible to witness. They were lively and open to suggestions. They were flowing with new ideas and shared different approaches that would benefit the project we were all working on. Sharing my love of color with them re-connected each woman in my office with her creative self, and that wonderful energy spilled forth as creative ideas in our meeting.

Creativity is sharing your inner world with the outer world.

When you do this whether it is the dinner you make for your family, or the power point presentation you made for the meeting, or the handout you made for your students - you are allowing your creativity to shine through and this creates a natural surplus of inner well being that supports you and everyone around you.

Creativity points

1. **Tune In** - Look around where you are sitting right now and write down everything that has been created by someone. Make a list (and it will be surprisingly long). Feel how each item on your list was once an idea, a thought, a feeling, and now it's there in front of you in physical form. Now write down three ideas that have been inside you, swirling around in your inner world for awhile. Look again at everything around you that once started from this same beginning phase. Close your eyes and now visualize your three ideas right there next to you in the physical world.

2. **Make it Simple** - What can you say or do right now in your current work environment that is an expression of your inner world? Send an email telling your boss your idea for the next marketing event. Make a sculpture out of paperclips. Draw a flower on a sticky note and post it on your computer. Take the colorful clip out of your hair and add it to your bulletin board. Make a masterpiece with your next cup of coffee by finding that unique palate of color you most want your coffee to look like—by adding just the right amount of sugar or cream. Make a cool looking swirl on the top with the wooden stir spoon. Go ahead and create a simple master piece.

3. **Support** - Look at the ground below your feet. Really feel the floor just below your shoes. You are supported. Feel into that support. You've probably never thought about it, but you're supported each day by the earth below you. Your creative ideas are automatically anchored in you through the ground under your feet. What you may not know is that to strengthen your creative inner spark, energy is pulled up from the earth through your feet to give the propulsion, and power to support your ideas. When you're ready to bring your creative ideas to fruition, call upon the energy from the earth. Visualize this power coming up through your feet to support you. Your creations will spring forth with ease.

Soul Doodles
by *Elizabeth Harper*

Whenever I feel inspired to draw what I call a Soul Doodle I know that some aspect of me wishes to communicate. A soul doodle or mandala—a Sanskrit word meaning both center and circumference—is a visual reflection of your inner world and your true self. Swiss psychiatrist Gustav Jung drew a daily mandala in his journal for the "soul" purpose of revealing his state of mind, spiritual development, and personal growth.

Surprisingly, we often do this unknowingly in the form of doodles that appear on first impression to be nothing but a series of mindless drawings. Yet the symbolism they depict can be both profound and revealing. Unlike ancient mandalas that were symmetrical and designed to attain higher consciousness through meditation, a soul doodle is drawn without pre-conceived notions of attaining any particular level of awareness. It can be symmetrical or asymmetrical and essentially contains colors, shapes and symbols that intuitively emerge from the soul. The focus is on a symbolic image of one's own energy, expressing the physical, mental, emotional, and spiritual worlds of your inner self. It captures thoughts, feelings, and sentiments and is in essence representative of an aspect of the soul.

I discovered that by drawing a mandala style of doodles I could connect with many different aspects of myself, all within one picture. As well as my past, present, and future self, I could also see a part of me that at times seems unavailable—my emotional self. This aided my understanding of situations I was unable to process. Because of this, my doodling has become an invaluable tool for transformation and one of the best ways to communicate with my soul.

Soul doodles are usually expressed in color over a white background and within the parameters, or thereabouts, of a large circle. A short meditation before drawing quiets the mind and creates a sacred space for the creative soul to communicate wisdom and guidance. A time is set usually around 20 minutes. Any longer and the mind can step in to edit the drawings.

Then, with the aid of colored pens or pencils, you begin intuitive doodling by filling the circle with whatever comes to mind, sometimes packing it with masses of energy and occasionally leaving it almost empty.

The following exercise will help you to draw your own soul doodle. You do not have to follow this, just go right ahead and draw whatever feels right to you. Your feelings are the clue to drawing a soul doodle. You may choose to draw houses, flowers, scenery, or symmetrical or asymmetrical shapes and patterns. You might fill the paper or leave most of it untouched; stay within the confines of a circle, or draw outside the lines. Allow yourself the luxury of playing with the communication of your soul. The more relaxed you are with this, the easier it will be.

Soul Doodling Exercise

Tools: Blank piece of white paper with a large circle drawn in the center, colored pens, paints, markers, crayons or pencils, a journal or extra paper to write on.

1. Put some soothing music on to help you to tap into your creative genius. Make yourself comfortable, close your eyes, and go through a relaxation process. Allow your body the comfort of relaxing. The more relaxed you are, the more in touch you will be with your soul light.
2. Ground and energize yourself by visualizing roots growing from the soles of your feet and going into the ground, connecting you to powerful magnetic earth energy. Bring this energy back up through your roots and into your heart. Next, visualize the sparkling, golden light of universal energy all around you. Draw this through the top of your head and connect it with the energy of the earth within your heart. Feel the wonderful glow of these two energies rejoicing as they join forces. Visualize your heart expanding with energy until you are surrounded by a warm glow, the glow of your open heart.

3. Sit for a short time in the energy, feeling relaxed and receptive, and then connect with your heart and ask it to communicate with you in pictures. Invite your soul to guide you as you select your first color. When you are ready, open your eyes and begin creating your soul doodle. Let go of all preconceived ideas about form and patterning; just allow the colors, symbols and patterns to speak to you in whichever way they come. If you think about it, the soul doodle will not be a true representation of your soul. Give yourself 20 minutes to complete your doodle, using your intuition to tell you when the picture is complete,
4. When you finish, close your eyes for a moment and ask for inspiration to understand the communication of your soul. Imagine your picture is a room you're walking into. How does it feel to be inside that room? What emotions, thoughts, and ideas emerge as you journey through the soul doodle? When you're ready open your eyes, write down any insights that came to you and then study your picture for no less than ten minutes. Write down any words that come to you—and that means *any* words, even if's something you need to go shopping for. Any thought can be relevant. Think about it afterwards rather than censoring your impressions.
5. When you feel you've received as much information as you can from your soul doodle, read through what you've written and arrange the words so they make sense. Allow your intuition to speak to you. Most importantly, be open to receive the information.
6. Finally, date your soul doodle and give it a title. Invite your soul to offer you guidance for the title.

Interpreting your doodle

When looking at a soul doodle, I find it useful to split the picture into portions: The left side of the picture represents the potential coming into your life, and the right side the influences moving out.

This information comes from my many years of experience seeing auras. The upper portions are mental and conscious, while the lower portions are emotional and subconscious. The midline represents the physical.

The outer edge of the soul doodle is the edge of your world, so whatever you put there represents your barriers or lack of them. As you study the symbols, realize it may not be the individual shapes that are important, but the whole picture. Your soul doodle is not supposed to be a work of art! It is a symbolic representation and will probably include a range of symbols, from recognizable images such as flowers, rainbows, and trees, to more obscure patterns including squares, triangles, and dots.

Your intuition is the best guide you have to understanding the communication of the soul. Whatever came to mind on first looking at your soul doodle is probably the most accurate interpretation you will receive.

Authenticity Exercises

Calling Your Energy Home: An Exercise in Restoring Authenticity to the Workplace
by *Deane Driscoll*

In our present uncertain economic times, many corporations are run in what I call crisis mode, which is about as bad as it sounds, especially you want to live your daily work life in a state of calm. With massive firings, temporary workforce hirings, reorganizations, downsizing through attrition, paying minimum wage (which is not actually a living wage anymore), and keeping weekly hours below full-time to prevent companies from having to pay healthcare and other benefits, today's work world is like a covert war being waged by corporations against the very employees who keep their businesses running. Having to live each day by putting out fires—or trying not to get burned—is not living at all. Worst of all, this kind of stress often separates us from our authentic selves: the singular voice we each have inside us that defines us.

What can an ordinary person do to stay calm and authentic at work? In the past I have worked in these crisis-oriented, high-stress environments and I didn't always handle the stress well. In fact, I can recall more than one occasion when the stress drove me to hyperventilate in the restroom. And having experienced this kind of pressure, I can tell you that when confronted with it, most people will either panic (ultimately joining in the fray), or become frozen and absent. When people freeze up, you'll see a sort of deer-in-the-headlights response when you look into their eyes. These folks are easy to recognize because they often spout the company line in lieu of speaking their own truth. And because stress is generally an either/or situation, a fight or flight type of response often follows.

So, you're either extremely present (but not necessarily authentic) and panicking, or you freeze up and either check out or shut down.

But there is a third option: to become a beacon of centeredness, a light in the proverbial dark.

I won't kid you—it's probably easier to stress out every day with your fellow colleagues or check out and hyperventilate in the restroom, than to work on inner calm. But the real downside of adding to the already overburdened stressed-out horde is that when you endure this kind of thing over long periods of time, you will eventually self-destruct. Or you hurt others by taking your stress load out on them. Or—and this is perhaps worst of all—you stop caring. You become as numb on the outside as you are stressed on the inside. This is bad. And you should avoid it. When people use the old adage "It's not personal, it's just business," they are really saying they're about to do something morally repugnant, but they don't want to take personal responsibility for it. They don't want to feel. They don't want to care. Being authentic can be hard work. So, at that point they disconnect and forget that we're all in this together.

But caring is ultimately what makes us human. Our shared humanity is what connects us. Caring isn't something to avoid at work; it's something that can make work better. Of course first, you have to care about *you*. And that means getting and staying centered. That means tuning into your authentic voice instead of trying to silence it. Mainly, it means taking control of your energy: the energy you allow in, as well as the energy you put back out there.

Becoming a beacon

So how can you access the third option? How can you become a beacon of calm and authenticity in a dark world? When I find that all around me is in complete and utter chaos, when the other employees (or even bosses) are stressed out to the point of crisis or panic, I carefully and deliberately stop what I'm doing and call my energy back home. Here's what that process looks like, step by step:

1. **Observe Yourself.** The first step is to notice that something is off, something is wrong. And it helps to notice this before you hit crisis mode. Early detection is the key. Notice your comfort level. If something is making you uncomfortable, don't ignore it. And one of the most important things to

take note of is when you say things or engage in behaviors that are not like you—something you wouldn't be proud to go home and tell your family about (like how you went off on your cube-mate and told him just where he could stick that report he was demanding from you). Ask yourself, "Was it my authentic voice that snapped so rudely at me co-worker, or did my own voice get drowned out by the voice of the stressed out hoard?" Remember that nothing will improve without self-knowledge, and nothing happens without your permission. Know what your real inner voice sounds like, and learn to recognize when the voice coming out of you isn't authentic.

2. **Stop yourself.** It's human nature to want to hit back when we feel hurt, abused, or stressed-out (crap rolls downhill, as the saying goes). But when we respond to ugly with more ugly nothing improves and we lock ourselves into a no-win situation. Do it often enough, and it becomes a habit. So, JUST SAY NO.

    Before responding in kind, just pull up and stop. Visually picture a wall or a STOP sign. Sometimes I like to just visualize a giant neon NO floating in space in front of me, like a ghostly note from God. As in, "NO, you cannot have my calm" or "NO, I will not be part of your crazy" (and you can't make me!). Just do whatever it takes to interrupt the chain.

3. **Direct your energy.** When people are about to go postal it's as if they're in a giant electrical storm and all their energies are scattered to the four winds. They're all over the place. They are not directing their energy because they are not consciously in control of it. And their energetic shrapnel is hitting innocent bystanders left and right. You can shield yourself from this fallout and use your own energy to make things better instead of worse. Here's how:

First notice that you're not trying to actually change the other guy. The other guy is presumably already stressed out, and stressed out people don't listen well. So don't try to stop others. Don't try to reason with people in crisis. They are in survival mode. Focus instead on yourself. And—bonus points—I found that if I can calm myself, my energy will often have a residual effect on everyone else as well, creating a sort of mini oasis of calm that surrounds me and positively affects those that wander into my wake.

In Step One you observed your own energy. Use that now. Become aware of your personal energy and how it is separate from the chaos all around you. Then direct (or redirect) that energy in whatever way you can. Move it. For instance: take three or four deep breaths; count to 10 (or 100 if your environment is really crazy); picture yourself on that beach you visited during your last vacation—or in your recliner with a gin and tonic if that's how you relax. Picture all your co-workers doing the watusi (laughter often helps). Whatever. Think of anything that will help you disconnect from the prevailing corporate winds and regain equilibrium and self-control. Once you can feel your energy, you can direct your energy. And that puts you in control.

4. **Call your energy home.** Now—and this is the real gem of the entire exercise—picture yourself as if you're in the eye of the storm, where everything is completely quiet and calm. Time seems to stop. For just a moment sound evaporates and you are completely alone and at peace. The storm still rages on all around you and you are aware of it, but you are no longer part of it. The idea here is to acknowledge the crazy going on is outside of you, but it can only enter your safe, centered place if you let it in. By withdrawing from the fray you protect yourself from all that energy swirling madly outside. You create a safe space in which to breathe, regroup, and forge a new energy pathway.

Personally, I like to visualize myself wearing Dorothy's ruby red slippers and clicking them together three times as I say, "Home, home, home." (Hey, don't judge me. So.... what's your favorite movie, Spiderman? Okay, then, picture the center of a web instead of shoes. Whatever works). The point is to mentally put yourself in your safe place, untouched by panic or fear or stress.

5, **Center yourself. Now pull in on your energy. Breathe deeply.** Feel your energy circling you. Wrap it around you like a warm cloak. Keep pulling in until the energy is back where it belongs; feel it enter your core, the very center of your being. After all, that's where your energy came from in the first place. Breathe it in, absorb it, glow with it. At the same time, picture white light at your feet and over your head. Draw this light energy up through the floor and down from the ceiling. Take it in and allow it to mix with your own energy. This is divine light, energy from the Source, and it will recharge you and keep you steady. This light is never-ending. It cannot be diminished if you use some up. It is there for you to use, whenever you need it, as much as you need. It will never run out. So just keep breathing. Feel your solar plexus growing stronger with each breath you take.

You are in control now. You are centered, grounded, and no outside force can throw you off balance while you are in this state. You are not a leaf on someone else's ill wind, to be blown hither and yon. You are an ancient tree, strong and steady, with roots that reach deep into the very core of the earth.

Now you are in the driver's seat, your energies will go where you direct them. No more automatic negative responses. No more hyperventilating. No more bosses or co-workers draining away your energies. You now have the self-control, inner calm and authenticity to choose how you want to react in any given situation. You are fully in tune with your own inner voice and have the power to react from your heart center. Because that's where your authentic self lives. Your own voice is now stronger than any voice outside of you. Listen to it. Then speak your own truth regardless of what others are saying. Follow your own inner guidance regardless of what others are doing.

Welcome home!

Mind Your Own Blissness with the Power of Play
by *Tam Veilleux*

Play is a state of mindfulness that often escapes us in this busy world. Too often we think that working harder will bring success at a faster rate. Chasing your tail will only make you dizzy, so unless you love that vertigo feeling, stop going in circles, slow down, and play.

The happiness and relaxation of playing allows your working mind to rest so new ideas can enter your consciousness. Science has proven that the more rested your brain is outwardly, the more active it is internally. Our cellular structure can expand and make room for new information when we let ourselves unwind from the burden of constantly seeking out connections. The ideas that slip into your playful mind often lead to above average results.

And the good news is, playing can be anything you enjoy most: power walks, baking the perfect loaf of bread, crossword puzzles, dancing in your office, window shopping, or a friendly Facebook chat. Know what works for you and occasionally allow your mind to slip out of work mode and into play mode, where you will be much more receptive to creative ideas and intuitive hits.

Your time-to-play jar

Create a list of fun things that feel like play. Have at least fifteen of items on the list, then cut them into strips with one method of play per piece of paper. Fold each paper and place them all inside a pretty jar or vase. The next time you find yourself in a funk, break out the *"Time-to-Play* jar and do whatever activity you pull out. Enjoy the endorphins, dopamine, and incredible ideas that arrive as you revel in the power of play.

Hint: If you can't think of fifteen fun things to do, start small. Here are a few common ideas:

- have a cup of hot chocolate
- take a refreshing bath
- get a massage
- go for a walk
- read a book you enjoy

Now you get idea! Keep this list handy and use it often, especially when you feel stressed.

Expressive Art Authenticity
by *Lynne McGhee*

In a world where over scheduling, overwork, and overwhelm are in abundance, we become disconnected from ourselves and what we need to create the life we want. As a fulfillment coach, I co-collaborate with my clients to illuminate the values, ideas, beliefs, and dreams they hold sacred. I help them shift the barriers of self-limiting thinking and perspectives so they can attain their goals and find greater happiness.

When we don't take time for ourselves or fully understand who we are and what we need, our values, ethics, and integrity can be compromised. Ultimately we're left feeling frustrated, and powerless. When we stand firm in our resolve, with clarity, mindfulness and conscious living, we choose to step into our greatest power.

This exercise will help you access deeper insights about yourself through an art project. Expressive arts combine drama, music, visual arts, and other creative processes to enhance personal growth. Although creative in nature, the process is meant to be experiential, thus it is *learning* we gain as we move from one modality to another.

Materials you will need:
Writing Paper
A pen
Oil pastels (or colored pencils, crayons, or colored markers)
Two sheets of blank heavy paper
A magazine
Scissors
Mod Podge glue (or a glue stick)

Let's get started!
1. Gather your materials within easily reach. Position yourself so you're physically comfortable. Be sure to work in a quiet space where you won't be disturbed.
2. Shut your eyes. Take in a deep breath through your nose on a five count. Hold your breath for ten seconds, and then slowly release it through your mouth for five seconds. Repeat this five times.

3. Pick up the magazine and begin searching for words and images that answer this question "What I value most about myself?"
4. Cut the images out of the magazine with the scissors and place them on the blank paper using the glue to secure them. Don't over think it! If an image calls to you, use it.
5. When you feel finished, put down the glue. Now **take at least three minutes** to observe the collage. Consider these questions as you look at it:

    "What does this picture say about me?"
    "Is there anything here that surprises me?"
    "What do I love about this?"
    "Is there something I want to add?"
    "What about it makes me feel special?"
    "Does this represent my values?"
    "What am I feeling?"

6. Now pick up the writing paper and pen and begin writing about the experience. Considering the questions you just looked at, what have you discovered? When you feel your writing is complete, put down the pen. Re-read what you wrote.
7. Now pick up the other blank sheet of paper and the oil pastels. Thinking about what you wrote, draw an image that represents *what you feel in this moment*. Allow yourself the freedom to do this without judgment.
8. Pick up your pen and writing paper again and write about what this experience has given you.

Take away question

"How will this self-discovery reflect the conscious choices I make moving forward?"

Luminosity Exercises

Automatic Writing /Journaling Exercise
by *Sunny Dawn Johnston*

These are simple exercises that will help you discover your purpose. They can be used daily, weekly, or any time you feel something is shifting within you and you need more clarity or guidance. This exercise can be done any time you feel the need for increased clarity or guidance. As I mentioned, your purpose is constantly changing as you change and grow and expand. So, this exercise may be helpful at any given time along your journey of life. Automatic writing will help you to be conscious of what is calling to you at this particular time in your life so you can live intentionally and consciously.

Let's begin:

- Create a space where you won't be interrupted for at least an hour. (No cell phone or computer allowed.) Have a couple of sheets of paper and a pen. No computer for this one, please.

- If you feel so guided, take a moment to ask the God of your understanding, your angels, spirit guides, or any other spiritual deities, for assistance in discovering your purpose. If this is new to you, you can ask Archangel Michael, who helps with Life Purpose and/or Archangel Uriel who helps with seeing the greater vision, for support and guidance.

- At the top of your paper, write: My purpose is . . .

- Now write anything and everything that comes into your awareness. Write without editing and without stopping. I call this stream of consciousness writing. It can be words, sentences, or phrases. You do not need to write complete sentences. As you write, observe your emotions and the feelings you have in your body.

- Continue writing until you either feel empty, over thirty minutes have passed, or you have a lot of emotion.

- Go through your list and mark the items that brought up the most emotion in you—the things you could feel in your heart. The ones that resonated with you. The ones that made you cry. The ones that gave you chills. These messages, words, and sentences are our purpose.

So now that you have the words, you will know what your purpose is ... for now.

Reintroduction to Crystals & Stones
by *Dede Eaton*

As children, many of us are drawn to rocks. Deep inside, we inherently know and sense that they are special. We don't question this *knowing*, we simply collect pretty and interesting stones where ever we go; the beach, lake even the playground. It makes us happy, simple as that. Remember that feeling–being curious, experiencing wonder, and living in the moment? Some of us went on to study geology and have an official rock collection. Most of us lost interest at some point and our rocks were thrown away or given back to nature. Maybe we saved a few special ones as souvenirs from a family outing or vacation, holding special childhood memories.

When we begin or enhance our spiritual journey, seeking tools to expand our awareness, many of us are re-introduced to crystals and stones. If a long held interest and love for stones has been lingering dormant deep inside you, now is the time to explore that interest again. They have been awaiting your return to the magick and mystery that is the mineral kingdom. Our rock friends are available to assist us on this journey to self-discovery. The study of minerals can be a lifelong pursuit, sure to bring many hours of joy, learning, and enlightenment.

All stones and crystals have unique properties and characteristics. Things such as shape, formation, location, combining stones, and more can affect, enhance and amplify the energy of each particular stone or crystal. They can be enlisted to heighten our spiritual development, heal physical ailments, bring a sense of peace and calm to our lives, and lead us to deeper understanding of ourselves.

Always use crystals and stones with the best of intentions and deep gratitude; treat them respectfully as friends and a support team. The mineral kingdom is available to assist on many levels; spiritually, emotionally, and physically. The possibilities are infinite. We can employ the power and support of crystals and stones in a variety of simple ways:

Keep small tumbled stones in your pocket
Wear them as jewelry
Place them in your environment
Hold one, or surround yourself, during meditation to create sacred space
Create a crystal grid.

You may want to start a crystal journal to record your experiences. Here are some basics of working with stones and crystals to get you started:

Selecting your stones

Trust your intuition! You will "just know." You may want to do research before shopping and consider your purpose. But keep in mind that often a stone will make itself known to you when it wasn't necessarily what you were looking for. They choose us!

- Close your eyes, draw in a few deep cleansing breaths and place your hand over the stones or crystals. Allow yourself to feel the energy; you may feel a tingle or *ping* of warm or cool energy.

- Use a pendulum to help you choose. Determine "yes" and "no" with your pendulum, then place it over each stone while asking, 'Is this the appropriate stone for me at this time?'

- Flip through or allow a stone book to fall open randomly, letting you know what stone is currently calling to assist you at this time. (Similar to a "Bible Dip").

- Sit in meditation, allowing a crystal or stone to make itself known to you.

- It is best to purchase from a reputable seller—someone who cares and is educated about the source, energy, and quality of crystals. Be discerning; more expensive is not always better quality.

- Cleansing, clearing, and charging your stones:

- Crystals and stones carry residual energy for a variety of reasons: location, handling, people, and environment. You'll need to clean and clear stones before using them to work with you and your particular purpose.

Gently clean your stone or crystal with a dry soft cloth or brush and/or warm water, a gentle cleanser, and a soft brush to remove any dirt of debris. Be careful not to scratch or damage your stone or crystal. Some stones are not water soluble, so check before you begin. Depending on where the stones were acquired, some may require deeper cleaning using oxalic acid. Further research and the guidance of a professional geologist is advised.

Methods for clearing stones and crystals

Clearing methods include, but are not limited to: Water, Earth, Smudging, Salt, Breath, Sun, Moon, Nature and Ritual. Let your process be as simple or elaborate as you wish. You may combine several methods together. Intent is key; employ the method that works best for you while indicating to your stones that they will now be cleared of any unwanted, unneeded, unnecessary energy. Trust your intuition to know when they are cleared. Always be mindful of the type of stone or crystal you're clearing. Some methods will scratch or damage the surface. Check that they are water soluble. When in doubt, use a non-invasive method.

- **Smudging:** Waft sage, sweet grass, frankincense or your favorite incense over your stones. (smudge yourself too while you're at it!)
- **Earth:** Place your stone in the ground or a container of soil, uncovered or lightly covered.
- **Salt:** Place your stones in a bowl of sea salt. Sea or Himalayan salt is preferred due their clear energy signature, but table salt will do in a pinch. Glass, wood, or other natural material is preferred for the bowl; avoid plastic or metal if possible. Use salt alone or with spring water.

- **Water:** Hold or place in a mesh bag; place under moving water. You can make it part of your ritual to visit the ocean, or a lake, river or stream. If unable to travel, use the kitchen or bathroom sink or try a crystal bath.
- **Sun/Moon:** Place in or on a safe and appropriate container, basket or tray and leave in a safe location outdoors for an entire sun-moon cycle. Be cautious of fading. Placing your stones out during the full moon is also an effective and powerful method.
- **Breath:** Simply place your stone in your cupped hands and breathe on it. This is the Native American way.

Charging, activating and programming crystals

- **Charging:** Place crystals in the sun to absorb ultra violet rays. Bring to sacred place, and/or place in moving water.
- **Activating:** Spend quiet time with your crystal. Meditate and roll it in your hands, connecting energetically. Use techniques similar to clearing.
- **Programming:** Only quartz can be programmed for specific intent. It stores, amplifies and transmits energy. Quartz exhibits the properties of piezoelectricity and pyro-electricity. With Piezoelectricity, heat and light are produced with compression. Pyro electricity activates expansion when heated. (other stones have this property as well)

To program

- Write a thought/intent on paper. Place the crystal on the paper to absorb the thought.
- Hold the thought in your mind and breathe the thought into the crystal.

Drag and Drop
by *Sue Yarmey*

You are electromagnetic. If you could see yourself and had the right equipment, you would be aware of just how much light you emit. When you start adding the things people can see, like your smile and the sparkle in your eyes, you become incandescent!

If you've been spending your time with less that positive thoughts, repeated negative actions, or a general cranky attitude, then you, and the people around you, become aware (even without the right equipment) of how your light has dimmed. It's easy to turn it back up again. This exercise will help you change your electromagnetic signature.

I call this Drag and Drop. Think of your body as a giant computer with millions of files stored within your body memory. You are able to access all these files at any given time. The files you reference most often are on the surface, creating your electromagnetic signature. If you choose to change that signature, all you have to do is access other files, drag them from storage (your memory), and drop them into your "now" (your consciousness). If you're ready to let the world see how bright you are, you need to put your energy and attention on files that reflect your more sparkling personality. That means it's time to reference different files.

Find a memory from your past that brings back love, safety, fulfillment, joy, or other positive feelings. There is no one right memory. Don't worry about what was happening at the time. Instead, concentrate on how you felt in that moment. Find the memory. The feeling you're looking for is up to you. Once you know how you want to feel, you'll be able to find a memory that fits. Once you locate the memory, you'll be able to drag it to the surface, drop it into your "now" and change your electromagnetic signature.

This is best accomplished over a one week period. Each night for seven nights, as you drift off to sleep, recall the same memory you selected. Bring as many details into your process as possible—your age, what were you doing, who was with you, the weather, and other pertinent details. Tell yourself the story of this memory as a child would recite it—with that excited, spiral thinking, jumping from one thing to another.

When you can actually *feel* that feeling in your body, drop it into your "now" by saying, "This is how I feel about everything I do" or a similar phrase to fit your desire.

That's it. That's all you need to do. One week of thinking, feeling, telling the story, and placing it into your "now." After the week, just let it all go. What you've done is change your signal. Just as a radio station can change from one format to another, you've done the same. You are no longer sending out a signal that attracts a negative audience. You are sending out a new signal to attract a more positive audience.

Give it time and see what you attract. Pay attention. Keep your focus on your new remembered positive memory, and let the changes begin!

Mindfulness Exercises

Releasing Dissonant Feelings
by *Evelyn C. Rysdyk*

Excerpt from *Spirit Walking:
A Course in Shamanic Power* [18]

Negative feelings can cause DNA to wind tightly onto itself in what I call a DNA cramp. In this state, the DNA's ability to regulate cellular function or repair and replicate itself is impaired. This condition interferes with the health of the organism.

Laboratory analyses measuring the levels of SIgA (salivary immunoglobulin A), which is an easy-to-measure, immune system indicator, have proven that a ten-minute expression of anger or fear produces a six-hour decline in a test subject's immune response. On the other hand, when a ten-minute period of compassion, love, or gratitude is felt, there is a measurable six-hour boost in the immune system.

In addition, when you choose to generate coherent feelings of love, gratitude, appreciation, or compassion, you produce healing effects not only within your own body but also throughout the DNA-filled ecosystem.

Experiencing anger or fear is a natural reaction. It is also true that these feelings create disruption. We cannot simply suppress negative feelings, because unexpressed feelings are like a festering wound that continues to poison the body. In addition, when feelings are suppressed, we cannot harvest the information they're trying to provide. This may be more information about our situation or clues about the old wounds we still carry.

Learning how to receive the information our emotional body gives us and then releasing these disruptive feelings is a critical part

---

18 Evelyn C. Rysdyk, *Spirit Walking: A course in Shamanic Power*, Weiser Books (April 1, 2013).

of becoming a healthy and powerful spirit walker. Relieving a DNA cramp is an important step in developing mastery of your feelings and a first step in creative manifestation.

Exercise: Working with Fear and Anger— Releasing a DNA Cramp

Read through the exercise once or twice before you begin listening to the guided mp3 audio file that is freely available at **www.myspiritwalk.com** so you can gather the memories you will need to recall during the exercise.

1. Be still and begin breathing with a focus on your heart—as though your breaths originate in the center of your chest. Breathe for at least 10-15 breaths or until you feel yourself beginning to relax.
2. While continuing to breathe, remember a time when you felt grateful. It can be a feeling memory from the recent or distant past.
3. Allow yourself to fill with the feelings of that remembered moment.
4. Once you feel full of gratitude, allow those feelings to radiate from your body with each of your heartbeats.

Listen to this guided meditation and practice it at least twice daily, because developing emotional intelligence is necessary for becoming an effective shamanic practitioner. Practice until you can easily shift out of negative emotions anyplace and in any situation. I cannot stress enough how critically important this ability is to becoming a true healing force.

As you continue to practice this daily, keep a journal of what you realize about your own process. This is important, as self-knowledge is one of the keys to being a powerful shaman. Indeed, the mastery of our emotions is a crucial part of coming into harmony with the larger Harmony which we refer to as Divine and, therefore, critical for creating a new and beautiful model of life for yourself and your world.

Process questions
- Honestly ask yourself in what situations you are triggered into anger.
- What are your underlying fears? When do you believe they began?
- Think about how having emotional mastery could benefit your daily life. Record all that you discover.

Pratyahara: Withdrawal or Merging of the Senses
by *Suzanne Silvermoon*

Pratyahara is the withdrawal of the senses of cognition and action from both the external world and the images or impressions in the mind field. Sense withdrawal (pratyahara) rests on the solid foundation of a steady, comfortable meditation posture and smooth, deep, quiet breathing that has no pauses. The control of the senses closes off external stimulation and draws your consciousness away from images generated from the memory. Stopping the thoughts that arise in the mind is not your goal, although over time they will slow. In pratyahara we disengage from mental interaction with images or thought patterns, either external or internal.

Pratyahara is learning not to be disturbed by sounds, thoughts, feelings, vision and so on. Vision is easy to control as we can close our eyes, but how can we close our ears and skin? How can we learn to concentrate when we can hear cars, or birds, or the phone ringing? What about sensations on the skin like your hair tickling your face or even mosquito around your ankles? How can you even begin to concentrate if these things disturb you?

Ideally we want to master the senses so we can use them consciously and enjoy them when appropriate. We should have refined senses and take good care of them, but we must be careful not to become absorbed and locked up in them. Better to seek that which is of the highest experience: spiritual liberation. With this liberation comes immeasurable bliss and freedom.

Pratyahara is a way of living where we are not affected by outside stimulus in our lives. We should learn to restrain our sensory impressions on a day to day basis and also raise our pain threshold so we are able to tolerate discomfort and to distance ourselves from everyday mishaps. This will enable us to be less distracted by our senses until we eventually gain total control of our senses so we can concentrate (Dharana).

Over time, the practicing adept learns to turn away from the objects of external desire and instead seek the True Self. Once the practitioner has experienced the fullness of creation and the creator itself, the thirst for objects of the senses vanishes, because none compare to the ecstasy of knowing the True Self. It is said that the yogi prefers that which is bitter (intense spiritual practice) which in the end becomes sweet nectar. Others who are driven by their sense desires prefer that which seems sweet as nectar at first, but in the end will be as bitter poison.

Sense withdrawal practice

Begin to practice sense withdrawal practice by listening to sounds. With eyes closed, covered, or lights turned out, listen to all the sounds in your environment. Of all the sounds you can hear, choose to focus on the most subtle. As you improve your ability to focus your mind, the most subtle sound will become louder and louder. Then ask yourself, "Is there a more subtle sound beneath the one you are focusing on?" Shift your attention to this new sound until it becomes louder. Do not attempt to "not hear" the louder sounds. Let them come and go. They are of no consequence. Stay focused on the most subtle. As you step back further and further along this chain of sounds, you eventually hear your own breathing, and beneath that perhaps your heart, and beneath that... eventually you are hearing deep ethereal sounds, the sounds of consciousness. Of all of these ethereal sounds, which is the most subtle? Focus on that. Eventually, and with much practice, you may be able to hear the sound of creation. The echo left over from the big bang. When asked "what does that sound like"? The sages would reply AAAUUUMMM ... AAAUUUMMM ... AAAUUUMMM.

Mindfulness Through Conscious Dance
by *Lisa Holcomb*

"Dance like no one is watching" among a crowd of others or in the midst of laundry, dishes, even deadlines, and see what happens!

Music or no music, you can feel the vibration within you rise and release thoughts and tension, bringing you into the moment, a place of no thought, a place where you get out of your mind, into your body, and into *now*, an expansive blissful place.

Conscious Dance, what is it? What does it feel like? Conscious Dance is not structured, therefore it activates and builds your natural, organic, energy etheric body. Relaxation heals. This type of movement is for anyone, regardless of your dance skills or body type. It is soulful art in motion. For many this is a spiritual practice, because it places us completely into the moment, connected to a higher conscious state. Intuition is activated and us be present within the body, because we have a safe out of body experience. The term *conscious dance* was created in the last decade, although the practice is ancient.

Many people experience a taste of conscious dance when a favorite tune comes on the radio and you find yourself ecstatic, moving to the beat, filled with memories. Take those several steps further to ten, thirty, sixty even ninety minutes by yourself—or see if you can join a group dancers in your area.

BEGIN ON YOUR OWN

- Shoes off anywhere: living room rug, lawn, garden, office or class
- Deep breath, opening your eyes, arms, hands, and lungs
- Stretch yours fingers open as your hands drop beside you
- Surrender the day
- Head drops back
- Open your chest and yawn, bringing your hands over your head and reaching upward

- Unlock each shoulder, lengthening your spine.
- Eyes closed
- Collapse from your hips, hanging like a rag doll at your hips.
- Sway and bend at your knees
- Exhale
- Breath in (hanging there), exhale again
- Bend your knees closer into your chest.
- Wait as your spine realigns and adjusts, releasing tension.

DANCE
- Go to the floor or a chair
- Move, stretch and release your weight into the ground
- Trust your movement and let it lead you
- Notice yourself drift into a state of meditation
- Trust and let go

Group dances

Classes, or gatherings, take on a flow, much like a Yoga class that starts from floor up and back down again. What is different is the dance brings you into to a transformative, often called Shamanic state, then an incredible celebration of community and self, and finally back down again to relax. This flow activates an intuitive story the body wants to tell, by opening the etheric body, versus the mind, and releasing stagnate energy.

As you enter the dance floor, a crystal chandelier glows from above, softly illuminating faces and radiant bodies beaded with sweat. Fabrics fill the room with color, texture, and lightness. Taking a deep breath, people sway or swirl on the comfortable wood floor, stretching and waking up, to begin the dance.

Feet are donned in rhinestone leather dance thongs, duck tape, or in battered comfortable shoes. Enraptured with a rhythm that takes dancers out of their mind and into the moment, they effortlessly move to music, alone, together, or in a group. Bodies twirl and eyes meet, sometimes for a brief moment, other times for more. Sometimes the moment is like a magnet, where men and women find themselves flowing together as one, connecting with the vibe of an unknown force that moves and shapes them like soft clay. Each silhouette becomes a slide show of beautiful images, statues in motion.

Some of the most common known conscious dance classes nationwide include:

5Rhythms®, by Gabriel Roth;	Contact Improvisation, Steve Paxton;
Ecstatic Dance, Max Fathom;	JourneyDance™, Toni Bergin;
Dance Kinetics, YogaDance	Soul Motion, Dan Levin, and

One dancer and Kundalini Yoga teacher expressed it this way, "It is my journey into a blissful mystery!".

In contrast, well known traditional dance classes include: modern, jazz, ballet, hip hop and creative dance. These are similar to conscious dance in that they all illuminate the soul through movement. Traditional dance is different because it is structured with choreography.

Gymnasiums, church sanctuaries, yoga and traditional studios become temples, places to connect, disconnect, and share a moving meditation. No conversation is heard on the dance floor. There is only music, silence among dancers, and the expression of body language grounded in unconsciousness that becomes conscious. This community is a tribe, bound together in rhythm and movement to create wellbeing.

"The fastest way to still the mind is to move the body," says Gabriel Roth of 5Rythms®. This practice illuminates the soul. It is art in motion. It is a way to let go of heaviness, mentally and physically, giving you a glimpse into the innermost parts of yourself; your core qualities of calm connection; your Spirit. A place of acceptance and oneness. I look forward to sharing the dance floor with you!

Conscious Collaborators

To learn more about the skills and offerings of the conscious collaborators, please visit their websites:

David B. Goldstein	www.davidbgoldstein.com
Jennifer Crews	www.jennifercrews.com
Elizabeth Harper	www.sealedwithlove.com
Deane Driscoll	www.deanedriscoll.com
Tam Veilleux	www.tam-i-am.com
Lynne McGhee	www.lynnemcghee.com
Sunny Dawn Johnston	www.sunnydawnjohnston.com
Dede Eaton	www.themagickcloset.com
Sue Yarmey	www.sueyarmey.com
Evelyn C. Rysdyk	www.spiritpassages.com
Suzanne Silvermoon	www.indigolotusyoga.com
Lisa Holcomb	www.reflectiveartscenter.com

About the Author

DEB SNYDER IS AN INSPIRATIONAL SPEAKER, spiritual teacher, and the award winning author of four books. Her personal exploration into heart-centered living stems from her own unique experience with her daughter, Raegan Aria, who was born with a rare brain malformation. Raegan, who is nonverbal, used a form of energy communication to reach out to her highly intuitive mom in time of great medical crisis and thus saved her own life. After this amazing experience, Deb went on to study the science and theories behind energy. Her mission is to educate and inspire others to shine brightly.

Deb is the founder and executive director of The HeartGlow Center, a nonprofit charitable organization dedicated to honoring the sacred Light which shines within us all. We celebrate life! She is editor of *Inner Tapestry*, a holistic journal in publication in New England for nearly 15 years, which was recently donated to The HeartGlow Center to publish as a part of its charitable mission. *Inner Tapestry* is going digital in January 2015 and will feature writers, artists, and holistic experts from across the world.

Deb's formal education includes a degree in interpersonal communication and a Masters and Doctorate of Philosophy in Metaphysics. She is board certified holistic health practitioner. Deb focuses on bringing her methods and techniques to the world to inspire, promote healing, and enhance loving communication between people. Her articles on spirituality, intuition, telepathy and parenting have been featured in numerous magazines, websites, newsletters, and publications. She has been a featured radio guest on programs coast to coast. As an inspirational speaker and personal development teacher to groups large and small, she offers her heart-centered services in workshops worldwide.

You can learn more about Deb at her website: www.ignitecalm.com. To learn about Deb's charitable endeavors with The HeartGlow Center and *Inner Tapestry*, please visit: www.heartglow.org

CPSIA information can be obtained
at www.ICGtesting.com
Printed in the USA
FFOW05n1826081114